TECH MINDS

DIGITAL LITERACY & CODING TEXT BOOK | GRADE 8

8

This book belongs to..

Name : ....

Class: .... Section: .... Roll no.: ....

School: ....

SANDBOX

1000+ EXERCISES

MASTERCLASSES

CODE OLYMPICS

FILE STORAGE

ISBN: 979-8-88849-054-9

PREFACE

With the world around us getting increasingly digitized and revolutionized with wide adoption of technology, **it is only natural that digital literacy becomes part of the school education system.** Digital literacy enables one to effectively, safely and responsibly adopt technology and use it to efficiently solve complex problems. Developing understanding of how to leverage technology (through coding/programming) to find solutions is one of the most important and empowering skills that a kid can develop in their early years of education. **Learning to code develops not only computational thinking but also multiple other skills including problem solving, critical thinking, perseverance and enables growth mindset in kids.**

We already see technology finding innumerable applications in every field. As it becomes further ingrained in several important fields including medical, construction, finance, manufacturing, education etc., **the world would need more and more people skilled in the art of programming. Schools and parents need to realize this extensive opportunity and proactively invest in building computational and programming skills for their kids.**

The Ministry of Education has also given impetus to this in the last edition of National Education Policy (NEP). **NEP 2020 recommends coding, digital literacy and computational thinking as one of the essential skills that should be learned by all students** for them to be innovative and productive human beings. **CBSE has also taken a step ahead in this direction by introducing coding and data science as skill subjects for Grade 6 onwards** in a quest to prepare students for the 21st century skills. They have also advised on the **model coding curriculum** for grade 6th to 8th in collaboration with Microsoft.

This book completely incorporates the principles laid out in NEP 2020 and the guidance given by CBSE with respect to coding. The book will enable the kids/readers to gain a deeper understanding of technology and learn the basics of programming which will help them develop a deeper interest in advanced areas of computer science. **The book covers chapters on digital literacy, data science, web development, coding, programming and artificial intelligence.**

This book is a gateway for kids to get introduced to the world of technology and build a very strong foundation for becoming the innovators of tomorrow. We are open to any suggestions on how we could improve the book further.

TEAM CODEYOUNG 

INSPIRATION FOR THE BOOK

This book derives its inspiration from a thorough understanding of one of the most prevalent international standards for computer science – **K-12 Computer Science Framework led by ACM (Association of Computer Machinery), Code.org and Computer Science Teachers Association among others.** The standard recommends following concepts as being important for holistic computer science education - computing systems, networks and internet, data and analysis, algorithms and programming and ethics in programming. The book covers all the suggested concepts in varying levels of details as appropriate.

Section I	Chapter 1 & 2	Digital Literacy
Section II	Chapter 3 & 4	Web Development
Section III	Chapter 5,6 & 7	Algorithms & Programming
Section IV	Chapter 8	Artificial Intelligence & Machine Learning

This book has also made sincere efforts to incorporate suggestions laid out in the **National Education Policy, 2020 with regards to coding.** NEP 2020 recommends coding, digital literacy and computational thinking as **one of the essential skills** that should be learned by all students for them to be innovative and productive human beings. It also recognizes that **mathematics, computational thinking and coding need to be given more emphasis in schools** as it is identified to be critical for India's future and its global leadership. This book is an attempt to **enable students to develop all the above skills and help them develop deeper interest in the field of computer science.**

The book also draws inspiration from the **curriculum laid out by CBSE for coding.** CBSE released a suggested curriculum for Grade 6-8 to introduce concepts of coding using real life examples and keeping it fun and engaging through usage of block based programming. This book follows similar objectives and **uses a combination of block based programming and Python to introduce kids to coding concepts and strengthen them through applied exercises.**

Apart from this, **the team also did on-ground research with several teachers who teach computer science and programming** in reputed schools of India. The book incorporates most of the feedback received to **enable school teachers to further improve computer science education at schools.**

Acknowledgements

A lot of work from multiple people has gone behind to bring this book to life. While it might not be possible to cover everyone, we would like to thank the following people for the continuous efforts put in by them.

- **SUBJECT MATTER EXPERTS :**
  Rasik Gupta (B.Tech, PIET) and **Ashish Kumar (PhD- Chandigarh University)** for spending several hours in putting together content which covers the concepts in a language easily understood by kids

- **SECONDARY SUBJECT MATTER EXPERTS :**
  Neil Menezes (DU, Front End Developer) and **Charishma Reddy (PU, Software Developer)** for thorough technical review of the content.

- **PROJECT LEADERS:**
  Ashutosh Gupta (IIT Bombay, CU - Boulder) and **Mohit Khandelwal (BITS Pilani, IIM Bangalore)** for thorough pedagogical & curriculum research and content review.

- **PROGRAM MANAGER:**
  Kanika Sharma (MSc. - Chandigarh University) for curriculum research, structuring of the book and ensuring the book's vision is met on paper.

- **GRAPHIC DESIGNER:**
  Shamrudhaa P K (NIFT) for breathing life into the book through her design skills.

Finally, **"the founders"** of Codeyoung, **Rupika Taneja** and **Shailendra Dhakad,** for giving wings to the vision and turning it into reality.

We would also like to thank multiple school teachers from across the schools in India who were kind enough to share their feedback on the requirements and expectations from such a textbook.

Team Codeyoung 

Learning Resources

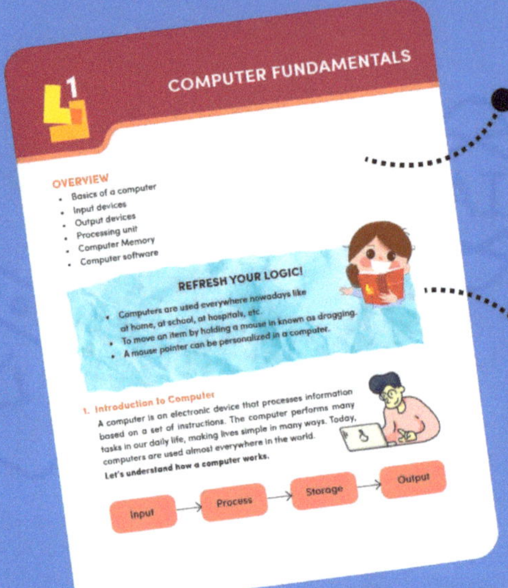

Overview

Get a quick summary of the key topics to be covered in the chapter

Refresh your logic

Refresh key concepts from the previous chapter which would be important for you to learn new concepts

Tech facts & Did you know

Get to know facts related to the field of technology

Tech Fact

The first version of HTML was launched in 1993 by Tim Berners-Lee

DID YOU KNOW

Supercomputers are high performance computers which are used for complex tasks like nuclear research and weather predictions. Their speed is very high as compared to general purpose

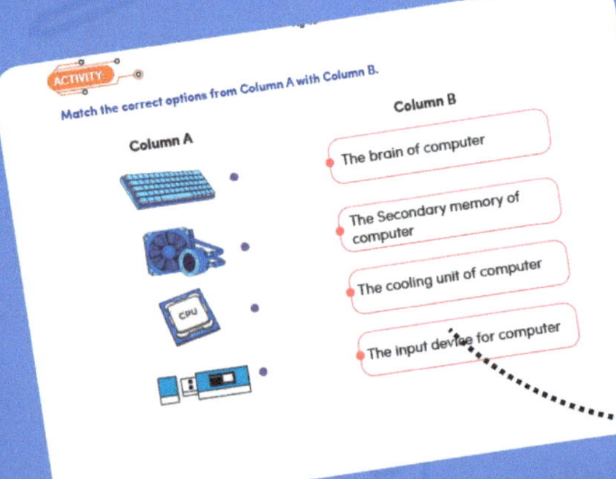

Activities

Strengthen understanding of concepts through hands-on exercises and activities

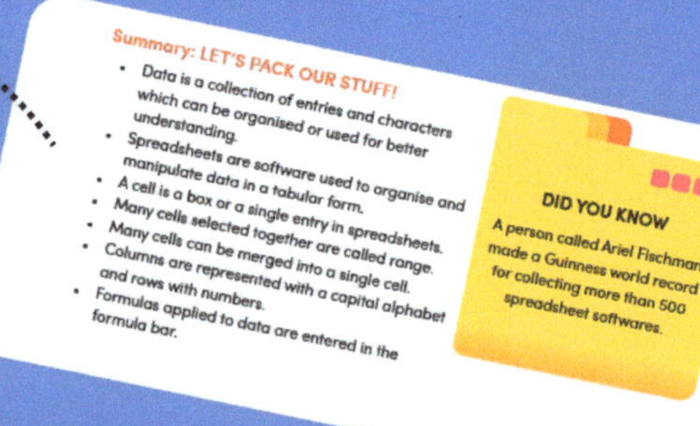

Summary

Quickly review everything you've learned in the chapter and refresh your understanding

Step up your code game

Test your coding and programming skills through an array of interesting questions and exercises

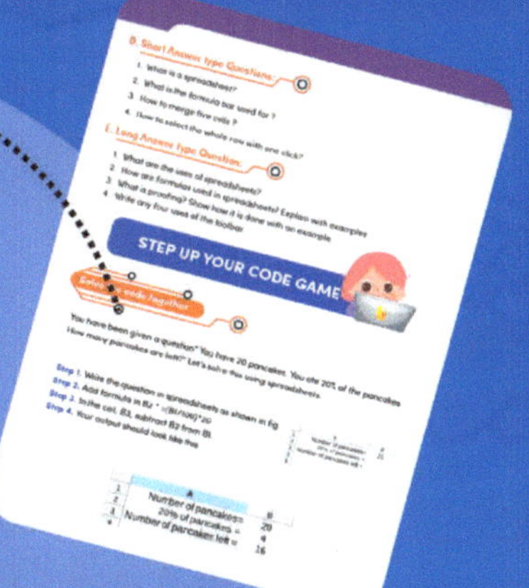

Compile your logic

Test your understanding and knowledge through different kinds of questions - fill in the blanks, MCQ's, True/False , short and long answer type questions.

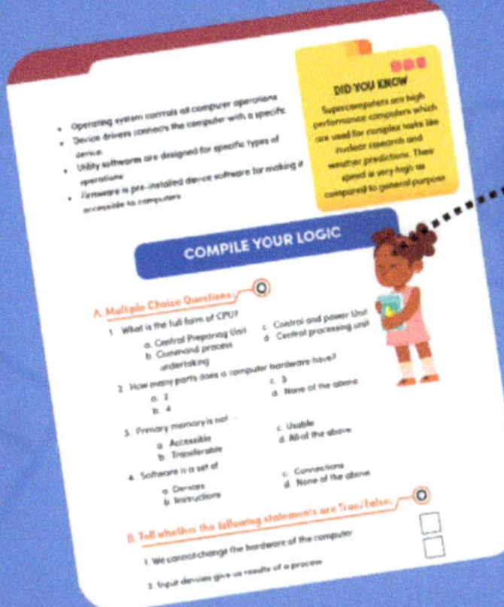

Explore the code

Solve the activity and understand the hands-on application of the concepts you have learnt in the chapter and uncover new ways of thinking.

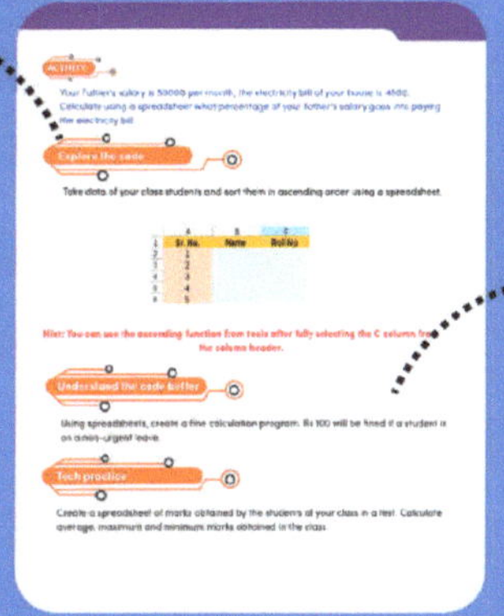

Understand the code better

Develop a deeper understanding of the concepts by independently solving a relatively tougher challenge

Decode the code

Login onto Sandbox, write your code and see the output spring up in front of your eyes - nothing as ecstatic as seeing your code work!

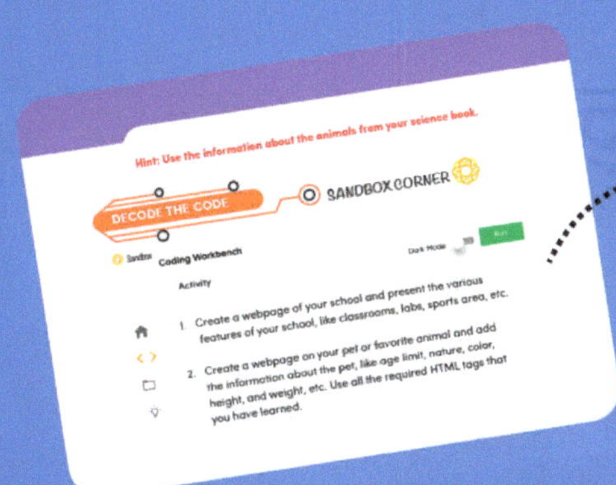

Master worksheet

Now it's time to test yourself with fill-ups, match the columns, intresting activities and have a check that you have mastered the sections

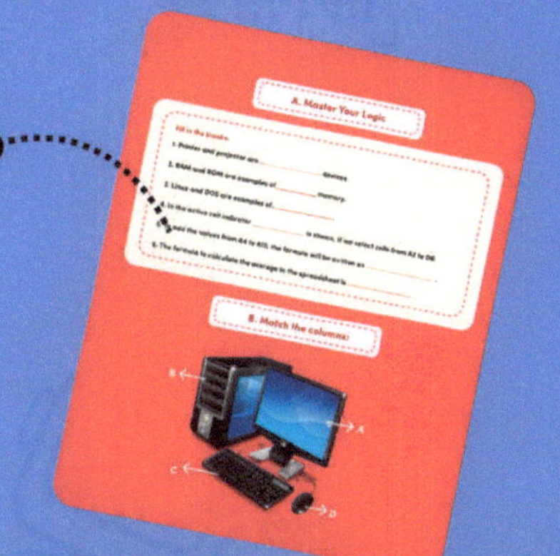

How to login to Sandbox?

Step 1 : Go to https://sandbox.codeyoung.com/#/

Step 2 - Click on Login as Guest

Step 3 : Enter you Email to start the registration

Step 4 - Proceed by entering your Name and Phone number (ensure it is a valid phone number as there will be an OTP verification)

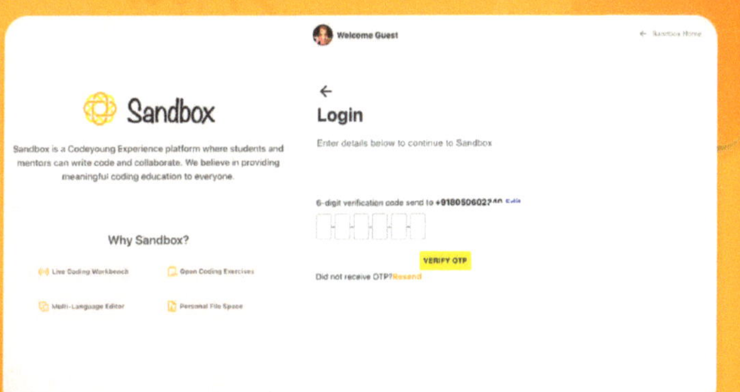

Step 5 - Once you proceed, complete the OTP verification and set your password

Step 6 - Once Password is set you'll be asked to login again with Email and set password

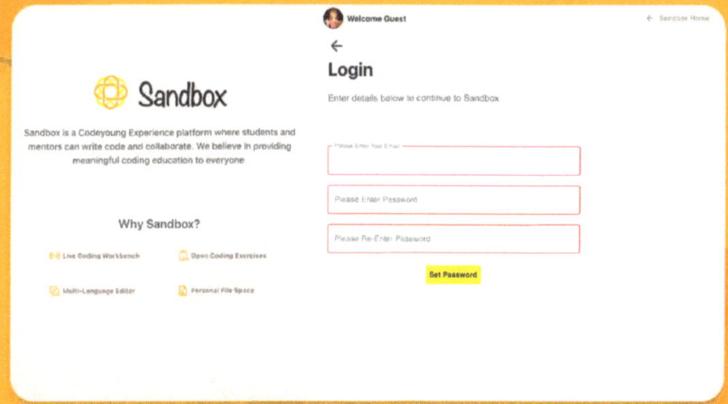

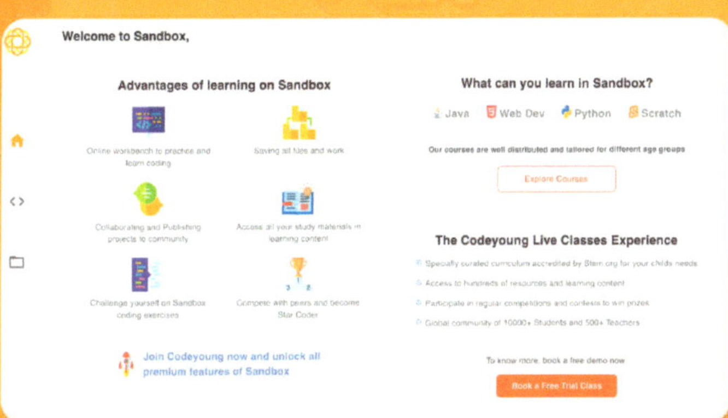

Step 7 - You are logged in to Sandbox and can explore the portal with navigation on the left hand side

How to unlock exercises on Sandbox?

Sandbox gives you access to 100s of exercises for different topics. To unlock the exercises, please follow the steps as mentioned below

Step 1: Login into Sandbox and go to the "Exercises" section

Step 2: Click on the locked exercise. It will open up a pop-up as shown. Please enter **"SBXGR8"** as the passcode to unlock all the exercises.

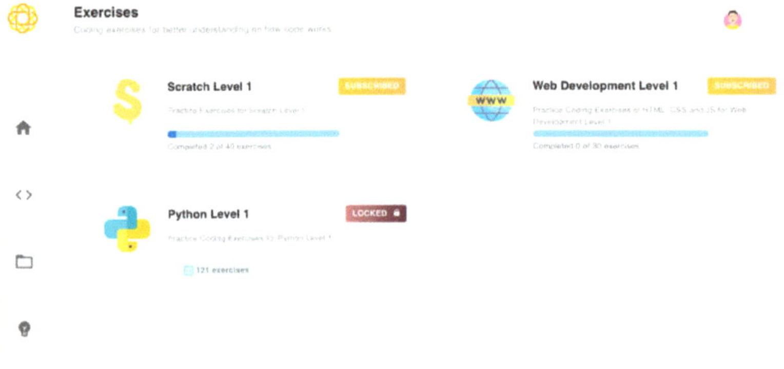

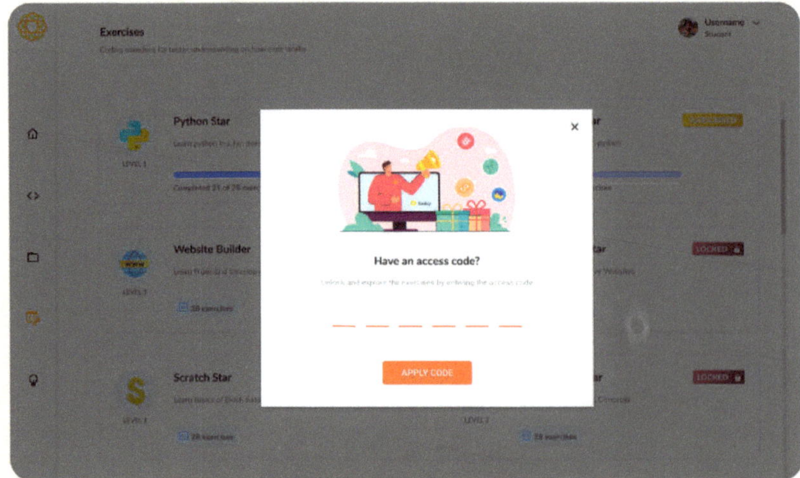

Table of Contents

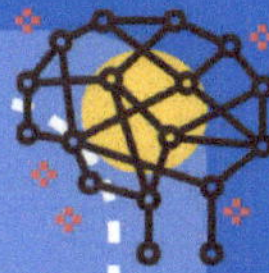

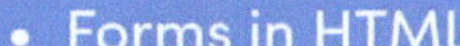

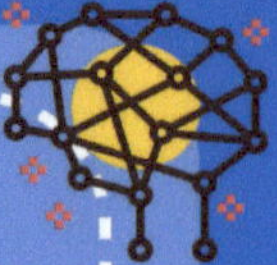

III. ALGORITHMS AND PROGRAMMING

IV. ARTIFICIAL INTELLIGENCE & MACHINE LEARNING

EXTRA RESOURCES

DIGITAL LITERACY

This section introduces kids to concepts of computing, networks and the internet, which would enable them to understand safe, responsible and effective use of technology. The second part of the section focuses on learning the art of data analysis.

1 CYBER SAFETY AND SECURITY

OVERVIEW

- Introduction to cyber security
- Need for cyber security
- Types of threats
- Safety tips to avoid cyber attacks
- Response to cyber attacks
- Ways to identify cyber attacks

REFRESH YOUR LOGIC!

- Computer network is the interconnection of multiple computing devices.
- The internet is used to access and share information all around the globe.
- The internet uses cloud storage to store data.

1. Introduction to cyber security

The Internet connects millions of devices around the globe and makes websites and data more accessible. Most of our data is available online. This also means that there are certain threats of data leakages or breaches.

When someone accesses information within the network without authorization, it is called **data breaching**.

Things that are related to the computer network, the internet, or internet data are termed **cyber**.

Hence, the practice of protecting networks or data from cyber attacks (like data breaching) is called **cyber security.** There are multiple rules in every country to counter cyber crimes.

Accessing information from a network without authorization is also more commonly known as **hacking**. The person who does this is called a **hacker**.

Hacking is of two types: Ethical hacking and Unethical hacking.
Ethical hacking is done to protect data from threats and attacks and is used to make networks more secure.
Unethical hacking is used by attackers to steal data or personal information.

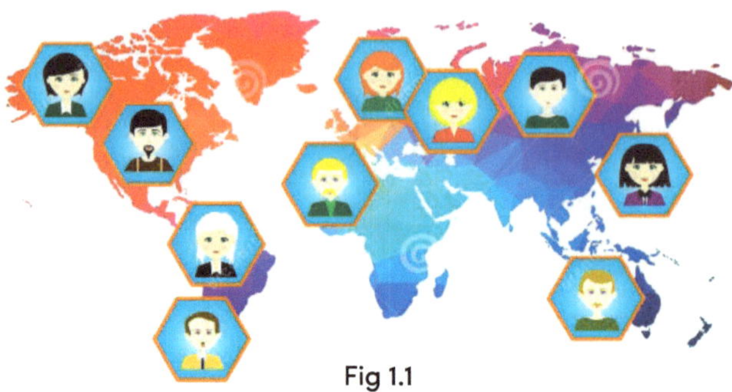

Fig 1.1

2. Need for cyber security

As online services are becoming more accessible, it is required that these services should provide security and safety of data. Cyber-security is important and needed for multiple reasons as listed below:

- It helps us protect information from external threats.

- It also protects information from internal threats by limiting access to users.

- It helps businesses to control the exposure of sensitive information to customers.

- Cyber attacks can reduce the performance of the network, and cyber security can help maintain the performance by protecting against such attacks.

- Cyber attacks can cost a huge monetary and reputation loss in case of loss of personal and sensitive data, and cyber security helps prevent that.

Fig 1.2

Tech Fact

Creeper was first virus designed to test ARPANET network.

- Customers trust brands with the most secure system. Hence investing in a secure system can help increase trust and in turn revenues for a company.

3. Types of threat

Hackers use different ways to access information without the user's knowledge or permission. These are broadly categorized into the following:

- **Virus**

Viruses are software specially designed to harm computer systems or networks. Viruses can replicate and modify other programs by inserting their own code. The name virus is derived from the biological virus. Like a biological virus, the computer virus needs a host program (host) to infect a system. It can generally enter the system through files shared from an infected system. There also exist computer worms that do not require any host program to enter the system.

- **Adware**

The pop-up advertisement that shows up on the computer screen while using a website or an application is called adware. These advertisements can contain viruses that can infect the systems. It installs itself without the user's consent and can record and send data about the user's activity. This in turn is used to target the user with other types of advertisements. The term 'malware' is also used for such software that is designed to harm a computer system.

- **Trojan Horse**

This term refers to the category of software that claim to perform a clearly defined function but in the background, they perform several malicious functions like using the microphone, camera, etc without the user's permission. Trojans can enter the system with a malicious attachment in an email or through a user clicking on some fake link or fake advertisements. It cannot spread like a virus but can help a virus to enter the system. It can control the system and can lock it completely.

Tech Fact

The name Trojan horse is based on ancient greek story "Trojan Horse" that led to the fall of the city of Troy.

- **Ransomware**

This category of software are used by hackers to take complete access of the user's devices and deny any kind of access to the user. The attacker then demands a ransom amount to unlock the system and give back the access to the user. Often, it also deletes its files after it gains access to the system files so that no one can crack its code. It can also threaten to delete or publish the data. Ransom attacks are mostly carried out using trojan software.

Tech Fact

'Wanna cry Ransom Attack'was a world-wide cyber attack in May 2017.
It affected more than 2M computers around the world.

ACTIVITY:

Match the type of threat with the cases.

Threat type	Cases
Ransomware	Your computer stops responding sometimes
Virus	You are not able to login into your device and get an email to pay some money to get access
Adware	A website using a camera or mic of your device without permission.
Trojan Horse	A website prompts a notification that "Your device is slow. Download this software to make it fast".

4. Safety tips to avoid cyber attacks

There are many ways you can keep your data safe from cyber attackers. Some of the ways are the following:

Fig 1.3

- Use strong passwords that are difficult to guess. Avoid using the same name and same password for every online account.
- Every update in software comes with an updated security. Keep software updated to avoid attacks.
- Avoid filling in personal and financial information on unknown websites or links to avoid any loss.
- Avoid downloading any unnecessary software from unauthorized websites to keep your system malware free.
- Use verified software that can detect viruses or malware in software and can delete them. This type of software is called **antivirus.**
- Always use a secured wireless network to share files and for making online payments.
- Keep yourself updated with the rules and regulations of cybersecurity.

Some of the cases of cyberattacks/attacks are given below. Fill in your response to save yourself from spam/threats.

1. An unknown person asks to use your phone.
Response – Say no!, they can steal your personal data.

2. A website asks to download random files.
Response – ____

3. A random person on call asks for your bank details.

Response – ____

4. In an email, you are informed that your bank account is locked.

Response – ____

5. Ways to identify and respond to threats

Always follow safety precautions to avoid threats. But if you still get some threats like spam emails or messages with links, there are several ways to identify them and respond correctly. Some of the ways to protect yourself are given as follows:

- **Verifying random or spam messages**

These sample messages from unidentified senders have come with links offering jobs or rewards. Always avoid clicking on such links or filling in any personal or fianancial information on any of the links provided by such unknown senders. Verify these links by checking the spellings of words used in links.

Earn Rs 8000-20000 per day easily, work online, no time limit, contact:http://wa.me/91827060125 KARTHIS E-COMMERCE PRIVATE LIMITED.

Play Rummy and Win Exciting Cash. Register for Free https://bit.ly/3bVOrDg & Get 2000* Welcome Bonus. T&C Apply

Fig 1.4

Response – Do not click on any link or fill in any personal information in these links. This will prevent attackers from installing viruses or stealing data from devices.

- **Spam emails**

Spam email are also very common. They contain links to products and rewards making it tempting to click on the link. These emails also use logos of popular shopping websites or banks (without any autorization) and ask you to fill in the details to claim rewards. Such emails are called phishing emails which collect your personal data and then sell them for money.

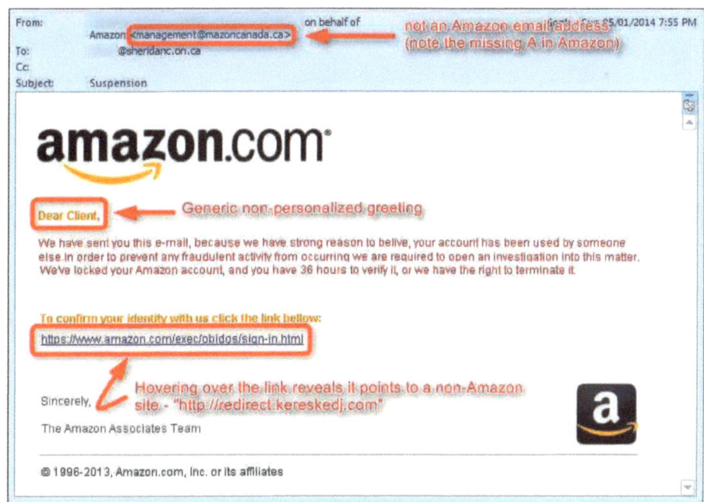

Fig 1.5

Response – Do not open these links or download any software or files from these links. These links can help attackers to install trojan software. Block such senders and mark these emails as spam to avoid them in the future.

- **Verify website links**

All website links start with **HTTP (HyperText Transfer Protocol) or HTTPS** (the additional 's' stands for secure). Websites that start with **"https"** use a protected system making them more secure and less likely to be attacked. Even though some links might seem to be secure , they can redirect users to unsecured links. Hence, always check the link before clicking on them

Response – Do not click on unsecured links. Never sign up on websites which feel fake or not secure. These websites are the primary source of viruses.

- **Spam calls**

Scammers use an unknown number to call a person and pretend to be an employee of a prestigious company or bank. They ask you some questions to gain your trust and eventually ask for your bank details. No banks or companies call their customers to verify personal details and hence these type of calls are almost always a scam which should be avoided.

Response – If you receive any spam calls ,do not provide any personal information and cut the call immediately. Also, report that number and block it.

Sam receives an email with subject "Winging money of ₹ 6500 can be updated in your Rummy account. Login id and get it fast!" but he can't see the full message. Should he click on the link to see full information? Also write the reason for your choice.

Winging money of Rs 6500 can be updated in your Rummy account, Login id and get it fast...! D Spam ×

Successful notification@airpostmail.in via mailmx1.acrossmail.com   Tue, Sep 20, 6:23 PM
to me ▾

Why is this message in spam? It is similar to messages that were identified as spam in the past.

Report not spam

If you cannot view this message, CLICK HERE

Should he click here?

Answer ____

Reason ____

REFRESH YOUR LOGIC!

- Cyber security deals with the protection of data from cyber attacks.
- Phishing messages are the most common way used by attackers.
- Ethical hacking is used to protect data from attacks.
- There are several laws to protect the public from online attacks.

Summary: LET'S PACK OUR STUFF!

- Cyber word is used for things related to the computer network, internet, and data.
- Accessing information without authorization is called hacking.
- Hacking is of two types: ethical and unethical.
- Viruses are software designed to harm a computer system.
- Trojans are software that perform a secret function in the background.
- Phishing refers to sending spam emails, messages, etc. to get personal information without authorization

COMPILE YOUR LOGIC

A. Multiple Choice Questions:

1. What is the primary aim of cyber security?

   a. Stealing data
   b. Storing data
   c. Protecting data
   d. None of the above

2. Adware consists of

   a. Unwanted emails
   b. Spam calls
   c. Pop-up advertisements
   d. Software

3. Which one is not a type of cyber threat?

   a. Virus
   b. Antivirus
   c. Malware
   d. Phishing email

4. In HTTPS, 'S' stands for

   a. Spam
   b. Standard
   c. Statement
   d. Secure

1. Antivirus can keep you safe from threats. ☐

2. Ransomware can lock the data of users. ☐

3. Trojans can replicate themselves. ☐

4. There are different rules in each country for protection against cyber threats. ☐

C. Fill in the blanks:

1. _______________ is an unauthorized access to data.

2. _______________ are software designed to harm a computer system.

3. Sending spam emails or messages is called _______________.

4. HTTP stands for _______________.

D. Short Answer type Questions:

1. What is ethical hacking?

2. What is cyber security?

3. What is malware?

4. What is a trojan horse?

E. Long Answer type Questions:

1. Why is cyber security needed?

2. What are the various types of cyber threats? Explain any three.

3. Explain various ways to avoid cyber attacks.

4. How to check an email for threats? Explain.

STEP UP YOUR CODE GAME

Some links are given below as received in emails and messages. Sort them into trusted and untrusted links.

1.   https://mail.google.com/   (________)
2.   http://mail.gooogle.com/   (________)
3.   http://wa.me/91730006721/   (________)
4.   http://2ff.fun/YY/G8xvm4M/   (________)
5.   https://www.codeyoung.com/   (________)

Hint: Websites with wrong spellings can be spam links.

Sam has received a message from an unknown person which says that he has won a jackpot worth $40000. Help Sam in identifying the spam/fraud in the message. Also, how should he respond to such messages?

Your friend receives an email from a sender "business.news@biorythmfree.com" and subject "Shoppers Stop Giveway". In the email, it is mentioned that his email address has been selected for a reward of ₹50,000 Rs and asks him to click a button in the email to unlock the offer. Is this a spam email? if yes, then list down the spam indications.

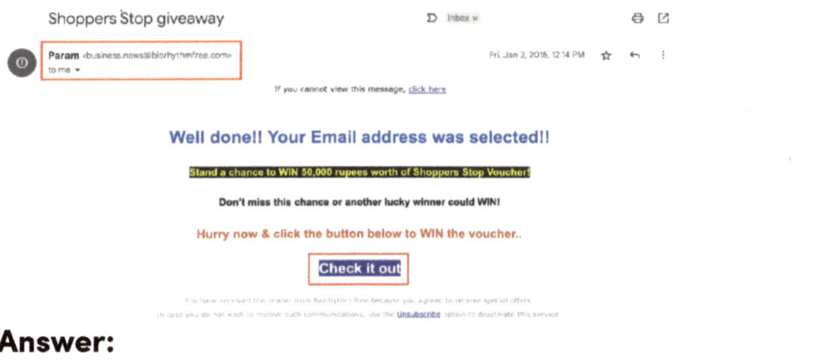

Answer: ____

Hint: Check the sender details and email id.

2. DATA TRANSFORMATION IN SPREADSHEET

OVERVIEW

- Introduction to data transformation
- Need for data transformation
- Techniques of transformation
- Transforming data using spreadsheet
- Challenges in data transformation

REFRESH YOUR LOGIC!

- Data is the collection of discrete values which gives information.
- Data visualization is a graphical representation of data.
- Spreadsheets are software used to manage data in various formats.

1. Introduction to Data Transformation

The process of transforming data from one format to another format is called data transformation. For example, conversion of document files (i.e. docs) into **portable document format** (i.e. .pdf) or converting a photo from **portable network graphics** (PNG) to **joint photographic experts group** (JPEG).

Data transformation plays a very critical role in data analysis. When we deal with a large amount of data, we might need to convert data from one format to another to enable its use for different analysis and illustration tools.

So, more accurately "**data transformation**" is the process of converting data from one form to another in order to make it more useful for analysis and to illustrate information given in data in a much better way.

2. Benefits of data transformation

Transformation of data is used in many fields for a better understanding of data and making it more useful for analysis. Some of the benefits are listed below:

- Data is transformed to make it better organized.
- Transformed data can be easily understandable for humans as well as computers.
- Use of data for different analysis may require data to be transformed into many different formats.
- Proper formatting of data can increase the quality and use of data.
- Data transformation increases the compatibility between data and the system.
- Data transformation can help perform faster queries on data.

3. Techniques of data transformation

Data can be transformed into many formats depending on the application of data. Transformation can be done in many different ways. Following are the ways generally used to perform data transformation:

- **Data Smoothing**

The process of removing distorted and meaningless data from data is called data smoothing. This technique is used to remove outliers and find patterns in data.

- **Data Aggregation**

The collection of data from various sources and storing it in a single format for further analysis is referred to as data aggregation. The quality and quantity of data and sources affect the analyzed output. Gathering quality data in large quantities from trusted sources is critical to get the better results.

- **Data Discretization**

This technique is used to divide large data sets into smaller data sets. The accuracy of data analysis can increase with the division of data into smaller groups. As the analysis of larger data sets requires much more time and effort, data discretization can help reduce errors and improve the efficiency of the analysis.

- **Generalization**

It is used to create more broad categories of data or to see a more generalized picture of trends and patterns in data.

- **Normalization**

Normalization of data involves the conversion of data variables into a specific range for efficient extraction of information from data for specific applications.

4. Transforming data using spreadsheet

Data transformation is primarily done using spreadsheets because the interface is very easy to understand and use. To perform data transformation, we are going to use LibreOffice calc spreadsheet software. Download the software using the link given below:

https://www.libreoffice.org/download/download-libreoffice

After downloading, install the software and open it. You will see the window as shown in the figure below:

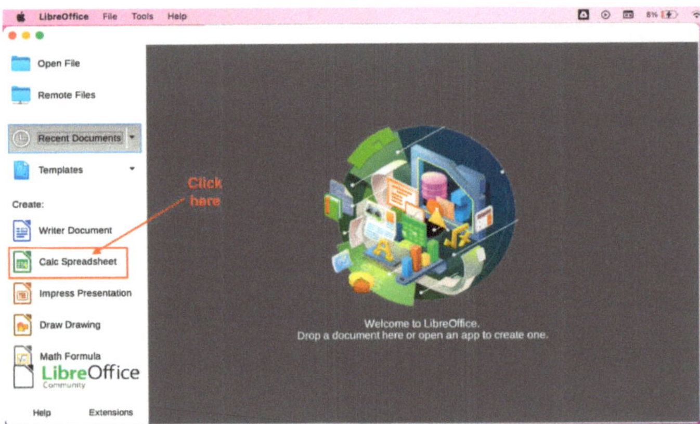

Fig 2.1

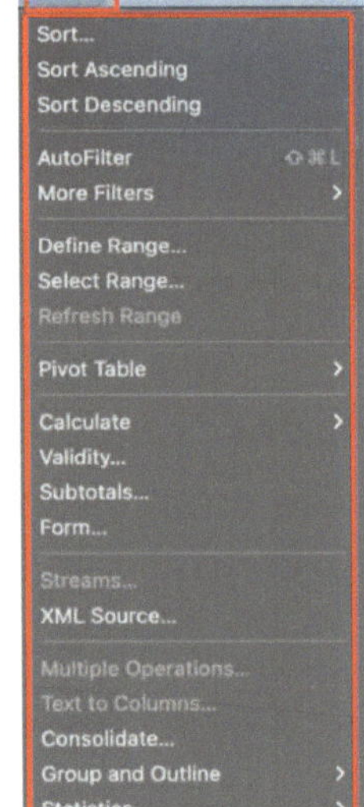

Fig 2.2

Click on the "calc" spreadsheet to open the spreadsheet.

Most data transformation tools are available in data options in the menu bar as shown in the figure.

There are several types of operations used for data transformation as discussed above. In this chapter, we shall use only a few basic functions which are used to perform the transformation of data.

- ## Sorting

Sorting is used to arrange data into a meaningful order for better analysis, i.e. ascending, descending or in a specific order. For example, arranging data of students according to their roll number.

A school is organizing a cricket training camp for students of class 6 to class 8. The data collected by the managing person is shown in the figure.

	A	B	C	D	E
1	name	class	roll no.	gender	Age
2	muskan singh	6	1	Female	11
3	ADITI	7	7	Female	12
4	SUNIDHI GUPTA	7	8	Female	13
5	kumar nitin	6	5	Male	12
6	Kriti	8	6	Female	14
7	JASWINDER KAUR	7	3	Female	12
8	rohit guleria	6	6	Male	12
9	AANCHAL	8	9	Female	13
10	nisha kanwar	6	2	Female	11
11	HARJAS SINGH	6	1	Male	12
12	muskan	7	5	Female	12
13	NIDHI	8	4	Female	13
14	neha chanu	6	9	Female	10
15	GUNGUN BHANDARI	8	3	Female	13

The above data looks unstructured and difficult to understand. So, let's perform some formatting changes followed by data sorting to make it better and easier to understand.

Step 1. Headings or legends of columns are not recognizable. To maken them prominent, we need to make them bold. To make them bold, select A1:E1 and press Ctrl+B. This will make all selected cells bold.

Step 2. Before performing sorting, we need to keep the first row in position. This ensures that when we do data sorting, data headers of the columns (the first row) will continue to remain at the top and not get sorted along with other data. To do that, go to **View > Freeze cells> Freeze First row.** This will keep the first row in place.

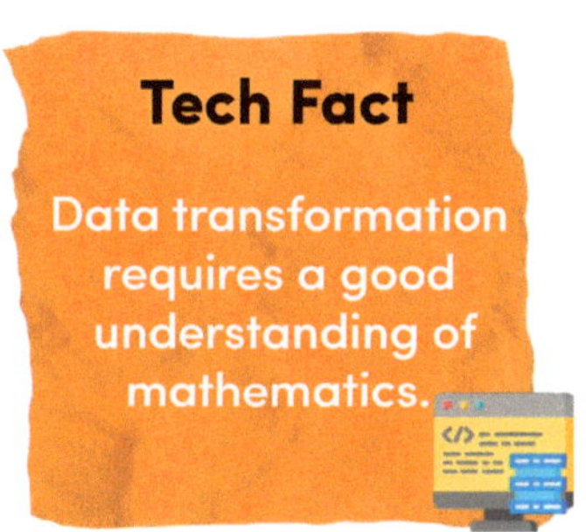

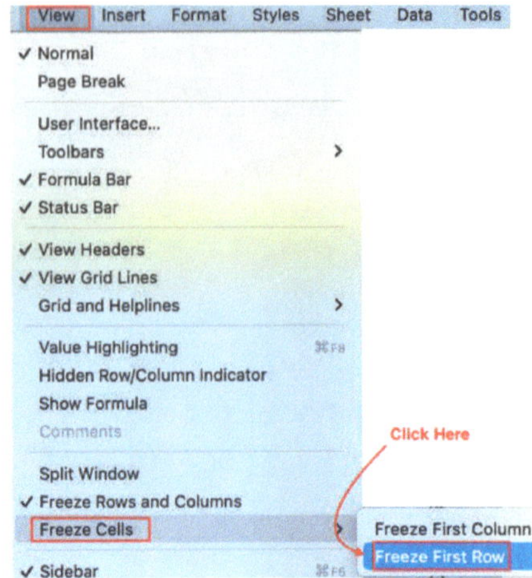

Step 3. Since the columns names are all in small case, let's capitalize those. Select the cells A1:E1. Go to **Format** in the **Menu** Bar and select **Text** then click on **Sentence Case**. This will capitalize the first letters of each column name.

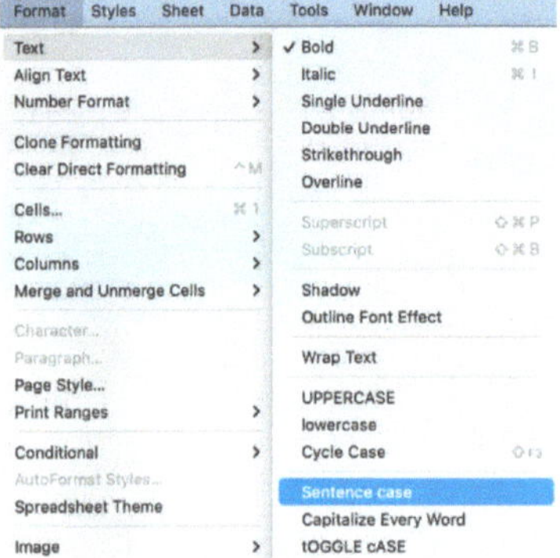

Step 4. Select whole data and centralize the text from the **Format** option – click on **Align Text** and then centralize (through '**Centered**' option) or directly press **ctrl + E.**

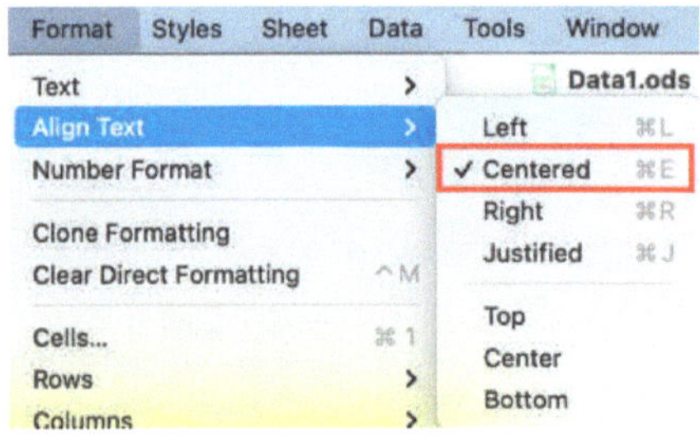

Step 5. Select column A and click on **Data** option and select the **Sort Ascending** option. This will sort all the entries in ascending order of the alphabet. Also, capitalize the first letter of each word in column-A using text format options (as used in Step 3)

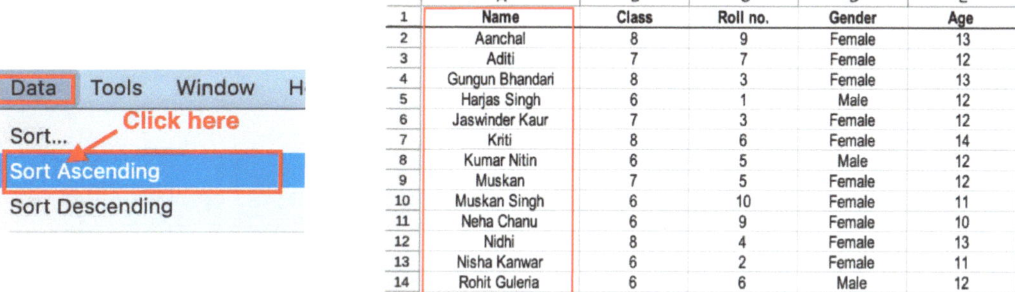

	A	B	C	D	E
1	Name	Class	Roll no.	Gender	Age
2	Aanchal	8	9	Female	13
3	Aditi	7	7	Female	12
4	Gungun Bhandari	8	3	Female	13
5	Harjas Singh	6	1	Male	12
6	Jaswinder Kaur	7	3	Female	12
7	Kriti	8	6	Female	14
8	Kumar Nitin	6	5	Male	12
9	Muskan	7	5	Female	12
10	Muskan Singh	6	10	Female	11
11	Neha Chanu	6	9	Female	10
12	Nidhi	8	4	Female	13
13	Nisha Kanwar	6	2	Female	11
14	Rohit Guleria	6	6	Male	12
15	Sunidhi Gupta	7	8	Female	13

Step 6. Add colors to your data to separate headings and the different entries. After doing formatting and data sorting, the data now looks better to understand as shown in the figure.

	A	B	C	D	E
1	Name	Class	Roll no.	Gender	Age
2	Aanchal	8	9	Female	13
3	Aditi	7	7	Female	12
4	Gungun Bhandari	8	3	Female	13
5	Harjas Singh	6	1	Male	12
6	Jaswinder Kaur	7	3	Female	12
7	Kriti	8	6	Female	14
8	Kumar Nitin	6	5	Male	12
9	Muskan	7	5	Female	12
10	Muskan Singh	6	1	Female	11
11	Neha Chanu	6	9	Female	10
12	Nidhi	8	4	Female	13
13	Nisha Kanwar	6	2	Female	11
14	Rohit Guleria	6	6	Male	12
15	Sunidhi Gupta	7	8	Female	13

- ## Grouping

When two or more columns or rows are grouped to divide them into separate categories, it is called grouping. This helps in displaying or hiding the grouped content.

Let's perform grouping on the data of the above activity.

For the training camp, candidates will be notified on next steps by their class teacher. Arrange the data into three class groups and hide the age and gender columns.

Step 1. Select the Class column and sort it in ascending order using sort options from data.

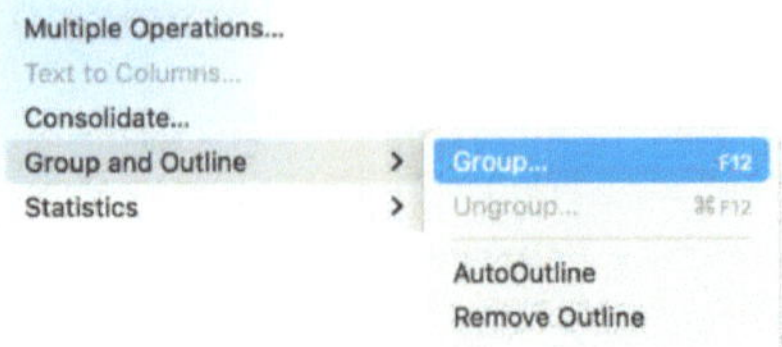

Step 2. Select all the rows corresponding to class 6 (row-2 to row-7). Go to **Data** option and click on "**Group and Outline**" and click on **Group**. Do the same for class 7 and 8.

Step 3. Now group columns D and E using the same method. The spreadsheet will look like this.

	A	B	C	D	E
1	**Name**	**Class**	**Roll no.**	**Gender**	**Age**
2	Harjas Singh	6	1	Male	12
3	Kumar Nitin	6	5	Male	12
4	Muskan Singh	6	10	Female	11
5	Neha Chanu	6	9	Female	10
6	Nisha Kanwar	6	2	Female	11
7	Rohit Guleria	6	6	Male	12
8	Aditi	7	7	Female	12
9	Jaswinder Kaur	7	3	Female	12
10	Muskan	7	5	Female	12
11	Sunidhi Gupta	7	8	Female	13
12	Aanchal	8	9	Female	13
13	Gungun Bhandari	8	3	Female	13
14	Kriti	8	6	Female	14
15	Nidhi	8	4	Female	13
16					

Step 4. Click on (–)minus signs to hide the data and (+)plus signs to show data.

Step 5. If we only want to show the details of students from class 6, then close all the groups and only open the one corresponding to class 6. The spreadsheet will look like this:

	A	B	C	F
1	**Name**	**Class**	**Roll no.**	
2	Harjas Singh	6	1	
3	Kumar Nitin	6	5	
4	Muskan Singh	6	10	
5	Neha Chanu	6	9	
6	Nisha Kanwar	6	2	
7	Rohit Guleria	6	6	
16				
17				

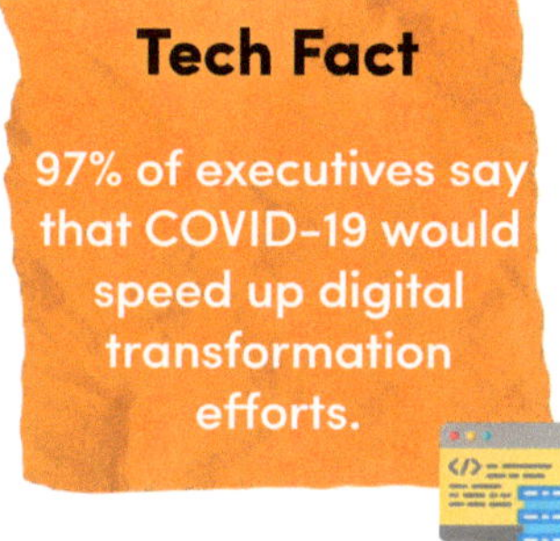

• Filters

Filters are used on a large amount of data for better visualization and analysis. When we need to cut the data to show only small and specific parts of the data, we use a filter to do that.

Let's use the filter on previous data to see how filters work.

During the camp, every student's details are verified or checked. Use the filters to find the name of a particular student to see and verify their details.

Step 1. Add the data from the previous activity into the spreadsheet.

Step 2. Select one cell from the data and then go to **Data** option and click on "**Auto filters**". On doing that, you will see downward arrows on each heading of the columns. These arrows are used to put the filter options.

	A	B	C	D	E
1	**Name**	**Class**	**Roll no.**	**Gender**	**Age**
2	Harjas Singh	6	1	Male	12
3	Kumar Nitin	6	5	Male	12
4	Muskan Singh	6	10	Female	11
5	Neha Chanu	6	9	Female	10
6	Nisha Kanwar	6	2	Female	11
7	Rohit Guleria	6	6	Male	12
8	Aditi	7	7	Female	12
9	Jaswinder Kaur	7	3	Female	12
10	Muskan	7	5	Female	12
11	Sunidhi Gupta	7	8	Female	13
12	Aanchal	8	9	Female	13
13	Gungun Bhandari	8	3	Female	13
14	Kriti	8	6	Female	14
15	Nidhi	8	4	Female	13

Before Filter

	A		B	C	D	E
1	**Name**	▼	**Class** ▼	**Roll no.** ▼	**Gender** ▼	**Age** ▼
2	Harjas Singh		6	1	Male	12
3	Kumar Nitin		6	5	Male	12
4	Muskan Singh		6	10	Female	11
5	Neha Chanu		6	9	Female	10
6	Nisha Kanwar		6	2	Female	11
7	Rohit Guleria		6	6	Male	12
8	Aditi		7	7	Female	12
9	Jaswinder Kaur		7	3	Female	12
10	Muskan		7	5	Female	12
11	Sunidhi Gupta		7	8	Female	13
12	Aanchal		8	9	Female	13
13	Gungun Bhandari		8	3	Female	13
14	Kriti		8	6	Female	14
15	Nidhi		8	4	Female	13

After Filter

Step 3. Click on the arrow in the name cell, and the filter options will be visible.

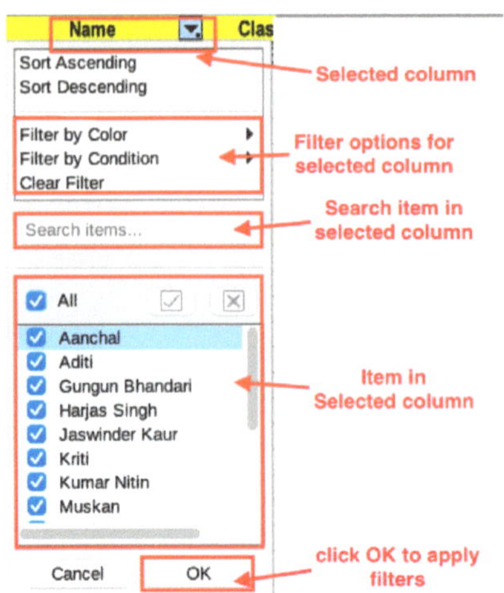

Step 4. Using the filter, we can search for a particular student. In the search option, write the name of the student whose details you want to find. E.g adding Muskan to the filter displays the details of the 2 students with "Muskan" in their name.

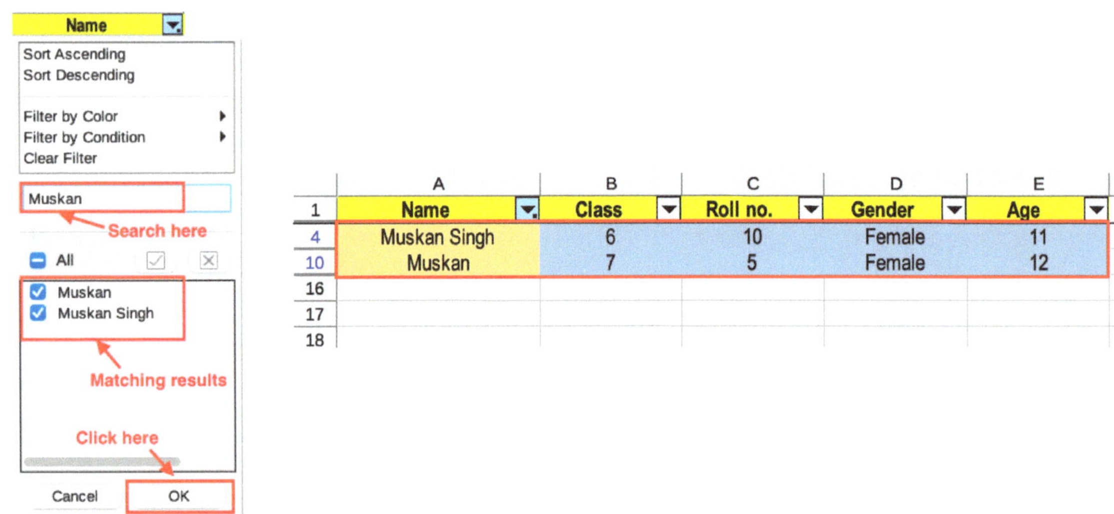

• Indexing and Matching

We use these two primary functions to find and match particular values in the data.

1. The index function is used to find the value from the selected range of data using row numbers and column numbers. The index function is written as:
   =INDEX (selected range, row number, column number)
   It returns the value of the cell which is present in the specific position.
   E.g. =INDEX(A1:E15,7,1) formula in the above cricket camp example, would return the value of cell A7 (7th row, 1st column) – "Rohit Guleria".

2. The matching function is used to match the entered value in a selected range of data (either a row or a column). It returns the row or the column number of the selected data range where the exact value is present.

=MATCH(value, lookup range, match type)

In this function, the match type is set at zero to find the exact match of the value. There could be other match types but for now let's focus on exact match.

Example, say we need to find "Sunidhi Gupta" in the name column in the above cricket camp example. Here the value is "Sunidhi Gupta", the lookup range is name column (A1:A15) and the match type is exact (which is zero). The formula would be: **=MATCH("Sunidhi Gupta,A1:A15,0)** – this would return **11** as the answer as Sunidhi Gupta name is the 11th row of the selected column. Similarly, replacing "Sunidhi Gupta" with "Aditi" would have given the answer as **8**.

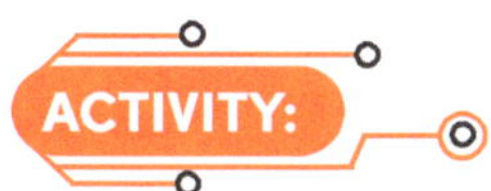

The following data table represents the marks obtained by students of a class in Mathematics, Physics and Chemistry test out of 20. Use the index and match function to show the marks obtained by a specific student.

	A	B	C	D	E	F	G
1	**Report card**						
2							
3	**Name**	**Mathematics**	**Physics**	**Chemistry**			
4	Harjas Singh	19	14	13			
5	Kumar Nitin	18	13	16		**Student's Report Card**	
6	Muskan Singh	14	13	13		Name	
7	Neha Chanu	10	10	14		Mathematics	
8	Nisha Kanwar	8	15	12		Physics	
9	Rohit Guleria	20	13	10		Chemistry	
10	Aditi	16	16	13			
11	Jaswinder Kaur	13	15	18			
12	Muskan	11	10	19			
13	Sunidhi Gupta	15	16	13			
14	Aanchal	17	17	16			
15	Gungun Bhandari	19	18	17			
16	Kriti	18	19	19			
17	Nidhi	15	15	11			
18							

Step 1. Enter the data in the spreadsheet as shown in the figure.

Step 2. Enter any name in cell "G6" from the name column. The name you put in G6 should exactly match one of the names in the table. What we want is that once a name of a student is entered in G6, the marks of the student in the three subjects (Maths, Physics and Chemistry) should display in the three cells below (G7, G8 and G9) respectively.

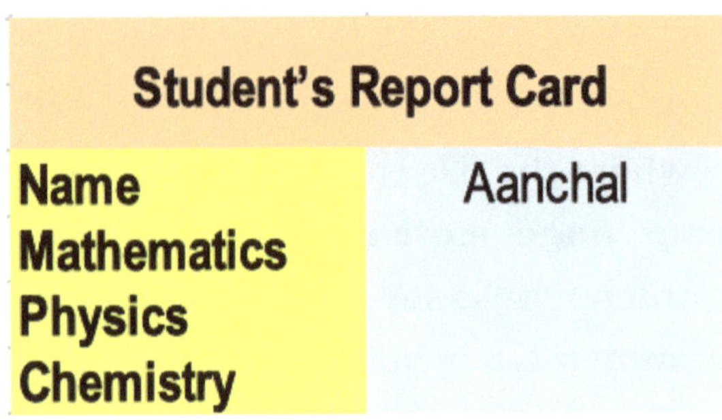

Step 3. Enter the following formula in cell "G7" (which corresponds to marks in Maths)

=INDEX(A3:D17, MATCH(G6,A3:A17,0), MATCH(F7,A3:D3,0))

In this formula, two formula have been used together to find the desired value. The column number and row number for the INDEX formula has been replaced by the MATCH formula as we need to find the row number corresponding to the name mentioned in G6 and column number corresponding to "Mathematics".

Step 4. In the INDEX function, **A3:D17** is the selected range of data to be used for indexing as that contains the required data.

	A	B	C	D	E
1					
2		**Report card**			
3	**Name**	**Mathematics**	**Physics**	**Chemistry**	
4	Harjas Singh	19	14	13	
5	Kumar Nitin	18	13	16	
6	Muskan Singh	14	13	13	
7	Neha Chanu	10	10	14	
8	Nisha Kanwar	8	15	12	
9	Rohit Guleria	SELECTED RANGE		10	
10	Aditi	16	16	13	
11	Jaswinder Kaur	13	15	18	
12	Muskan	11	10	19	
13	Sunidhi Gupta	15	16	13	
14	Aanchal	17	17	16	
15	Gungun Bhandari	19	18	17	
16	Kriti	18	19	19	
17	Nidhi	15	15	11	
18					

Step 5. At the row number in the index function, **MATCH(G6,A3:A17,0)** is used to find the row number of the value entered in cell G6 in the name column (i.e. A3: A17).

For example, if "Aanchal" name is added in the G6 column, then the MATCH formula would return 12 since "Aanchal" name is in the 12th row in the selected data range (A3:A17).

	A	B	C	D
1				
2		**Report card**		
3	**Name**	**Mathematics**	**Physics**	**Chemistry**
4	Harjas Singh	19	14	13
5	Kumar Nitin	18	13	16
6	Muskan Singh	14	13	13
7	Neha Chanu	10	10	14
8	Nisha Kanwar	8	15	12
9	RANGE FOR ROW MATCH	20	13	10
10		16	16	13
11	Jaswinder Kaur	13	15	18
12	Muskan	11	10	19
13	Sunidhi Gupta	15	16	13
14	Aanchal	17	17	16
15	Gungun Bhandari	19	18	17
16	Kriti	18	19	19
17	Nidhi	15	15	11
18				

Step 6. At the column number in the index function, **MATCH(F7,A3:D3,0)** is used to find the column number in the header row (i.e. A3:D3). Here, we need to find the column corresponding to "Mathematics", hence F7 cell is used as the value in the formula. The MATCH formula here returns the value as 2 as it's the 2nd column in the selected data range (A3:D3).

Report card			
Name	**Mathematics**	**Physics**	**Chemistry**
Harjas Singh	19	14	13
Kumar Nitin	18	13	16
Muskan Singh	14	13	13
Neha Chanu	10	10	14
Nisha Kanwar	8	15	12
Rohit Guleria	20	13	10
Aditi	16	16	13

Step 7. After applying the function, the value in the cell "G7" will return the value as 17. This is because the INDEX function now resolves as:

= INDEX(A3:D17,12,2) which leads to cell B14 and the value as 17.

	A	B	C	D	E	F	G
1							
2		Report card					
3	Name	Mathematics	Physics	Chemistry			
4	Harjas Singh	19	14	13			
5	Kumar Nitin	18	13	16			Student's Report Card
6	Muskan Singh	14	13	13			
7	Neha Chanu	10	10	14		Name	Aanchal
8	Nisha Kanwar	8	15	12		Mathematics	17
9	Rohit Guleria	20	13	10		Physics	
10	Aditi	16	16	13		Chemistry	
11	Jaswinder Kaur	13	15	18			
12	Muskan	11	10	19			
13	Sunidhi Gupta	15	16	13			
14	Aanchal	17	17	16			
15	Gungun Bhandari	19	18	17			
16	Kriti	18	19	19			
17	Nidhi	15	15	11			
18							

Step 8. Now select cell "G8" and "G9" and write similar formulas to get the results. Note that the only thing that would change in the formula would be the cells corresponding to the subjects. F7 cell which corresponded to Mathematics would change to F8 in the formula for Physics and to F9 for Chemistry. Rest will remain the same.

Student's Report Card	
Name	Aanchal
Mathematics	17
Physics	
Chemistry	

Student's Report Card	
Name	Aanchal
Mathematics	17
Physics	17
Chemistry	16

	A	B	C	D	E	F	G
1	**Report card**						
2							
3	**Name**	**Mathematics**	**Physics**	**Chemistry**			
4	Harjas Singh	19	14	13		**Student's Report Card**	
5	Kumar Nitin	18	13	16			
6	Muskan Singh	14	13	13		Name	Nidhi
7	Neha Chanu	10	10	14		Mathematics	15
8	Nisha Kanwar	8	15	12		Physics	15
9	Rohit Guleria	20	13	10		Chemistry	11
10	Aditi	16	16	13			
11	Jaswinder Kaur	13	15	18			
12	Muskan	11	10	19			
13	Sunidhi Gupta	15	16	13			
14	Aanchal	17	17	16			
15	Gungun Bhandari	19	18	17			
16	Kriti	18	19	19			
17	Nidhi	15	15	11			
18							

There are many other options for data transformation. You will learn more about them in further classes. We have taken very basic examples of data transformation here. But in real situations, data transformation is performed on very large data sets.

Converting data tables into charts or diagrams is also a form of data transformation. Data transformation can also be performed using coding languages.

5. Challenges in data transformation

There are several benefits of data transformation. However, performing data transformation comes with its own set of challenges as well. Some of them are as follows:

- Data transformation can be **expensive** since it requires specific systems, software, and tools to transform data, especially for large data sets. The main expenses come from computing resources, data sources, and the collection of data.

- The **authenticity of data** depends on the authenticity of sources. If data is collected from unauthentic sources, then the analyzed results will be invalid.

- Data transformation requires expertise in a specific field of data. A **lack of expertise** can result in an invalid output or an incomplete analysis. Also, it might cause the loss of important data.

- **Strategies for data analysis** play a major role in data transformation. Without a good strategy, the analysis can be incomplete or incorrect.

Summary: LET'S PACK OUR STUFF!

- Data transformation is a process to convert data from one format to another format for better and more efficient analysis.
- The main benefit of data transformation is to make data compatible for both humans and computers.
- Smoothing, aggregation, discretization, generalization, and normalization are techniques used to perform data transformation.
- There are many operations performed on data for transformation like sorting, filtering, grouping, etc.
- Main challenges in the transformation of data are cost, expertise, and authenticity of data sources.

A. Multiple Choice Questions:

1. Which one is not a type of data transformation?
   - a. Smoothing
   - b. Normalisation
   - c. Verification
   - d. None of the above

2. Ctrl + E is the shortcut for
   - a. highlighting data
   - b. editing data
   - c. centralizing data
   - d. None of the above

3. Which one is not a benefit of data transformation?
   - a. cost
   - b. compatibility
   - c. better analysis
   - d. none of the above

4. The shortcut for making text bold is
   - a. Ctrl+A
   - b. Ctrl+B
   - c. Ctrl+C
   - d. Ctrl+D

B. Tell whether the following statements are True/False:

1. Transformation of data is used to visualize data in graphical format.

2. Data transformation does not require data from valid sources.

3. Data transformation makes data hard to understand for humans.

4. Filters are used to analyze specific parts of data.

C. Fill in the blanks: 

1. Arranging data in descending order is a type of _________________ .

2. Smoothing is the removal of _________________from data.

3. Dividing data in smaller data sets is called _________________ .

4. Lack of expertise affects _________________ of data.

D. Short Answer type Questions: 

1. What is data transformation?
2. What is discretization?
3. Write the general formula for indexing.
4. How to select the whole row with one click?

E. Long Answer type Questions:

1. What are the benefits of data transformation?
2. What is indexing and matching?
3. What are the steps to sort data?
4. How do INDEX and MATCH functions work?

STEP UP YOUR CODE GAME

You are planning to live in a new city with your family. Your family has made a list of selected houses with rent. Sort the data into ascending order of rent amount and also write down the steps followed.

Houses	Rent amount (RS)
House 1	10000
House 2	12000
House 3	15000
House 4	11000
House 5	9500
House 6	10500
House 7	16000

Step 1. Enter the data into a spreadsheet.

Step 2. ____

Step 3. ____

Step 4. ____

Hint: Use functions from the data menu.

ACTIVITY:

Create a table of activities you do daily with the time spent in each of those activities.
Sort the data in decreasing order of time spent.

Activities	Time Spent

Explore the code

Make a table of your friend's name and their birth dates. Sort that data into ascending
order of birthday dates. Group friends' names who have birthdays in the same month.

Name	Birthday

Hint: Select the birthday column for sorting.

Make a list of items you wish to buy this year. Prepare a table of items in the format given below and group them into essential and non-essential items

Item name	Requirement

Hint: You can use sorting before grouping.

1. Collect data on your expenses for the month and sort them in descending order of amount.

2. Collect the data of scores/runs in a cricket match. Make a data table using spreadsheets. Then using formatting, find out who scored the highest runs.

Master Worksheet – Section 1

Master Your Logic

A. Fill in the blanks

1. A ________________ can replicate itself after entering the computer system.

2. ________________ hacking is used to gain unauthorised access to protect data.

3. The link to a secured website starts from ________________ .

4. A virus requires a ________________ program to enter a computer system.

5. Converting audio into text is a form of ________________ .

B. Match the columns

Column A	Column B
1. Smoothing	A. Dividing large data sets into smaller data sets
2. Discretization	B. Conversion of data variables into specific ranges
3. Generalisation	C. Collecting data
4. Normalisation	D. Creating broad categories of data
5. Aggregation	E. Removing meaningless data

Activity:

Sam sold train tickets at a railway station. The table represent the number of tickets sold per day for 10 days. Calculate the average number of tickets sold per day and also the total amount if Cost of one ticket is 25 Rs. Sort the data in descending order of amount.

	A	B	C
1	Day e	Ticket sold	Amount
2	Day 1	300	
3	Day 2	290	
4	Day 3	340	
5	Day 4	450	
6	Day 5	120	
7	Day 6	180	
8	Day 7	140	
9	Day 8	130	
10	Day 9	490	
11	Day 10	250	
12	Total		

Complete formula for cells from options

SUM, 25, (C2:C11), B10

C1 : =_ _ _ _*B2

C10 =25*_ _ _

B12 = _ _ _ _(B2:B11)

C12 =SUM_ _ _ _ _ _

Activity:

Following table shows the data on sweets preferred by a number of customers out of 1000 during the festival season. Arrange the data from most preferred to least preferred and also apply filters to find the preference of Jalebi.

Sweet	Number of customers
Gulab Jamun	200
Jalebi	140
Laddu	170
Barfi	160
Rasgulla	130
Rabri	100
Balushahi	100

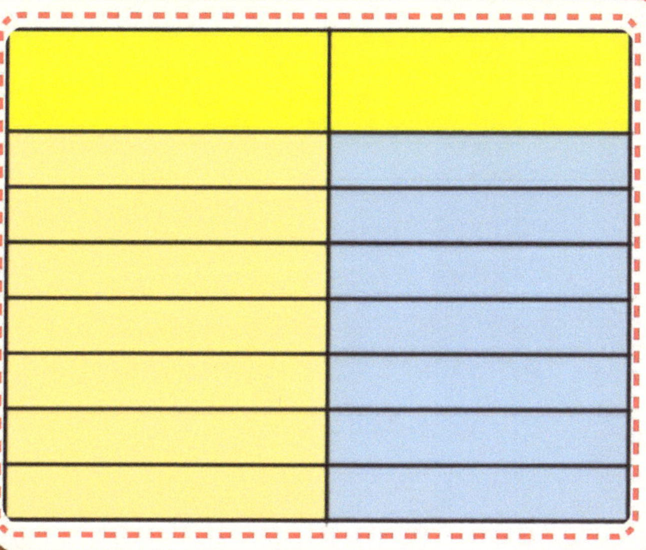

Challenge Your Logic

Activity:

In the following data table, different batteries and their capacities left out of 2500mAh are given. Calculate the percentage performance left, also apply filters on the table and arrange capacities in descending order.

Battery	Capacity(mAh)	Percentage capacity
Battery 1	2300	
Battery 2	2000	
Battery 3	1800	
Battery 4	2350	
Battery 5	1900	
Battery 6	2050	
Battery 7	2400	
Battery 8	1950	
Battery 9	1700	
Battery 10	1500	
Battery 11	2350	
Battery 12	2200	
Battery 13	2050	
Battery 14	1800	
Battery 15	2150	

Activity:
In the following images, Check if they contain unsecured links, if yes, then mark it.

1. Pricedetails You noticed for home-based labor. Now you can get up to Rs 20,000 per day. http://wa.me/919011003508 MAHALAXMISMSSERVICE

2. Dear Employeeyour Earn Rs 800-5000 per day easily, work online, no time limit, contact:http://wa.me/917319067219 RVPN

3. Exclusive offer! You are selected to Get free iPhone 13 on Membership so please check:- 1ji.me/p/fEfqM

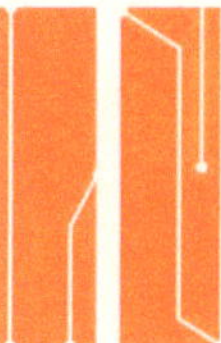

WEB DEVELOPMENT

This section introduces kids to the functioning of websites and how they can use HTML and CSS to build their own websites.

3 INTERACTIVE WEBPAGES

OVERVIEW

- Forms in HTML
- Borders and directions with CSS
- Class and ID selectors
- Div tag

REFRESH YOUR LOGIC!

- CSS can be written in three different ways, i.e., inline, internal, and external.
- A gradient background color can be given in three different ways, i.e., linear, radial, and conic.
- Font styling can be used as a property of CSS.
- Hover effect is used to apply a different property to the HTML tag using CSS.

1. Recap of HTML and CSS

While HTML is the backbone of the website and helps define its structure, CSS lets us add design and aesthetics to the website without impacting its functionality. A website can contain information like text, images, videos, audio, hyperlinks, etc., which can be styled by CSS using various properties.

As an exercise, create a web page using HTML and CSS for the webpage below:

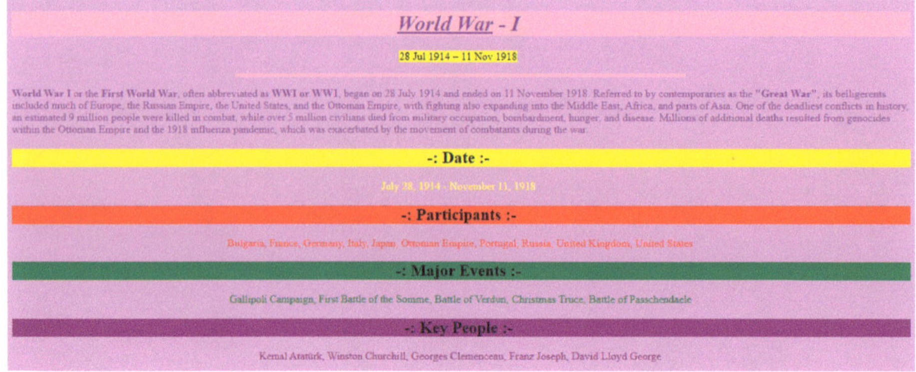

Fig 3.1

2. HTML forms

Forms in HTML are used to collect user information. Form is a container tag i.e. **<form></form>**, inside which all the input elements can be added.

To add text in a form, a **<label>** tag is used which is a container tag and used in the same way as acparagraph tag. To add any input element in a form, an **<input>** tag is used, which is an empty tag with various attributes.

The input tag has a **"type"** attribute that defines the type of information that has to be taken from the user. The information can be of different types.

Some common values of the type attribute are given below:

Input types	Description
<input type = "text">	To take single-line text information.
<input type = "radio">	Creates a radio button for choosing an option.
<input type = "checkbox">	Creates a checkbox to mark the various options.
<input type = "password">	To take input as a password.
<input type = "submit">	Creates a submit button for submitting the form.

Let's create a form to take some inputs from a user.

```
<html>
<head></head>
<body>
<form>
      <label><b>Full Name</b></label>
      <input type="text">
```

```html
        <br><br>
        <label><b>Gender:</b></label>
        <input type="radio">
        <label>Male</label>
        <input type="radio">
        <label>Female</label>
        <br><br>
        <input type="submit">
</form>
</body>
</html>
```

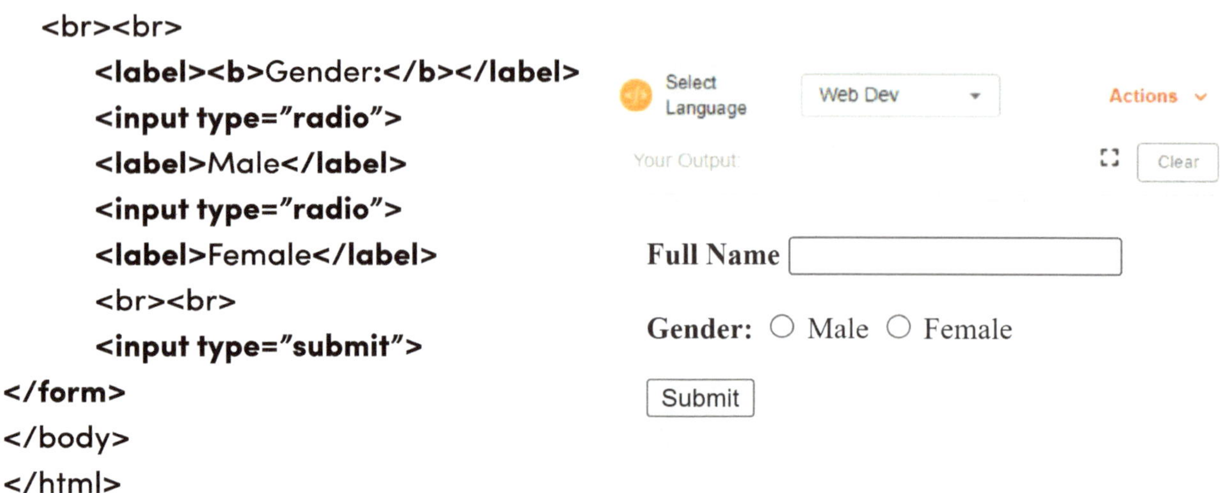

The form elements in HTML can be grouped in a box when they are enclosed in a
<fieldset> tag. A **<legend>** tag is also used to add heading to the box.
Let's group the elements and add a heading to the form:

```html
<html>
<head></head>
<body>
<form>
        <fieldset>
        <legend>Personal Details</legend>
        <label><b>Full Name</b></label>
        <input type="text">
<br><br>
    <label><b>Gender:</b></label>
        <input type="radio">
        <label>Male</label>
        <input type="radio">
        <label>Female</label>
        <br><br>
        <input type="submit">
        </fieldset>
</form>
</body>
</html>
```

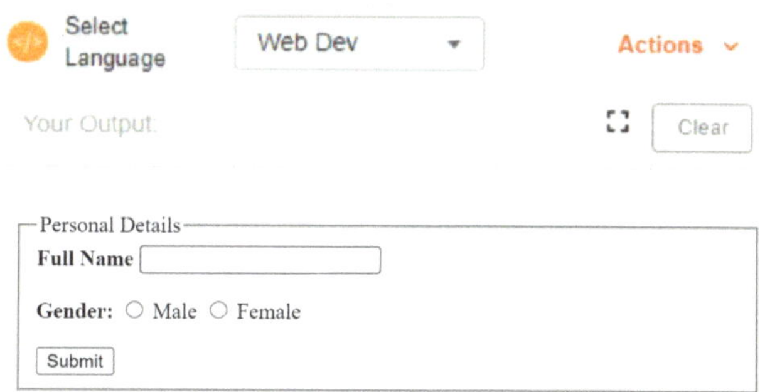

3. Borders and directions

To style any element of HTML with borders, the border-style CSS property is used with various values/attributes. The commonly used values or attributes of the border-style property are **dotted, solid, dashed, double, etc.**

The following example illustrates how to use border-style property (in the paragraph's CSS) to apply a border to a paragraph.

```
<html>
<head>
<style>
p { border-style: solid; }
</style>
</head>
<body>
<p>The paragraph is enclosed with a solid border</p>
</body>
</html>
```

> **Tech Fact**
>
> The border styling property of CSS can be used with any type of information in a website.

Output:

```
The paragraph is enclosed with a solid border
```

Border-width and Border-color are two different properties used with border-style to change the width and color of the border. Let's change the border color and width:

```
<html>
<head>
<style>
p {
border-style: solid;
        border-width:10px;
        border-color: red;
    }
```

```html
</style>
</head>
<body>
<p>The paragraph is enclosed with a solid border with different width and color</p>
</body>
</html>
```

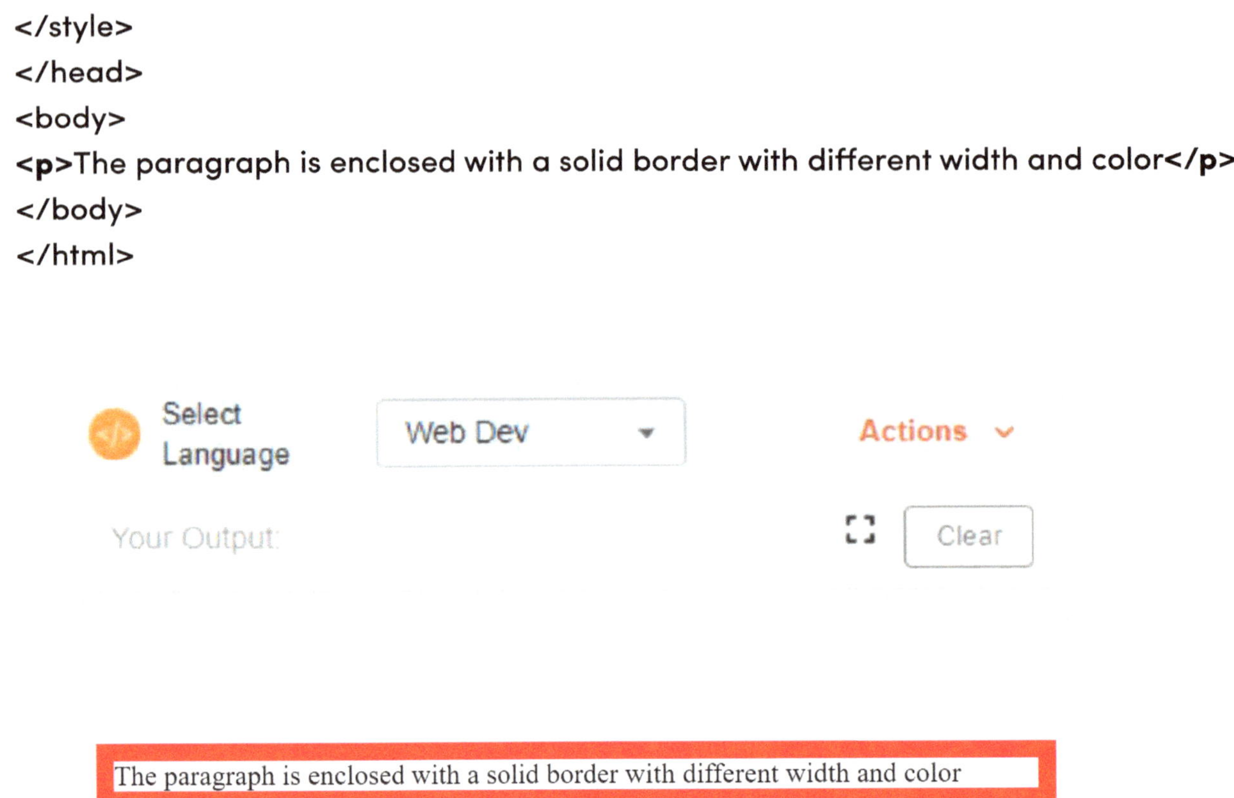

Direction property:

The direction property in CSS is used to change the writing direction of a text – this property can be applied to any text information like headings, paragraphs, etc. The default direction of writing text is left-to-right.

Syntax:
direction: ltr / rtl / initial / inherit;

The various values used with this property like ltr/rtl/initial/inherit are illustrated in the following table:

Values	Description
ltr	Text direction goes from left to right.
rtl	Text direction goes from right to left.
initial	Text direction sets to the default value.
inherit	Text direction is inherited from the parent element.

4. Class & ID in CSS

The class and ID are used as an attribute with the HTML elements. If several same types of elements/tags exist on a website, then class and ID properties are used to provide a unique identity to an element/tag.

The values of class and ID can be any alphanumeric or alphabetic values. It must contain at least one character, should not start with a number or contain whitespaces (spaces, tabs, etc.).

To create a CSS selector for ID, the symbol **hash(#)** is used with the selector name, and to create a selector for class, the symbol **dot(.)** is used with the selector name.

Let's create an ID and a class for the HTML elements/tags:

```
<html>
<head>
<style>
  p{
    background-image: linear-gradient(to left, yellow, white);
    border-style: dotted;
  }
  .a{
    color: red;
  }
  #x{
    color: green;
  }
```

```
</style>
</head>
<body>
   <p class = "a">This is the first paragraph of the website</p>
   <p id = "x">This is the second paragraph of the website</p>
</body>
</html>
```


5. Div tag

The div tag is used for grouping multiple elements/tags that the CSS can style. It is a container tag for an HTML document.

For example,

```
<html>
<head>
<style>
      div {
            color: purple;
            background-color: cyan;
            }
      p {
```

```
      color: purple;
      background-color: cyan;
    }
</style>
</head>
<body>
<div>
<p>The first paragraph of a div tag</p>
<p>The second paragraph of a div tag</p>
</div>
<p>The first paragraph without div</p>
<p>The second paragraph without div</p>
</body>
</html>
```

Tech Fact

The Div tag is also known as division tag without any division functionality.

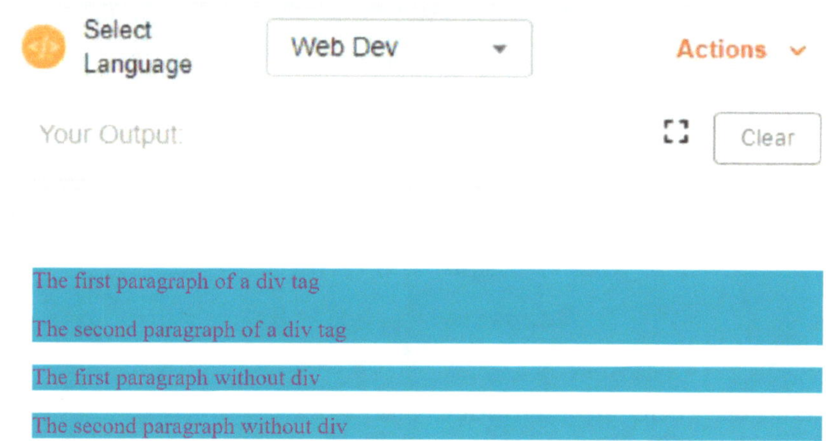

REFRESH YOUR LOGIC!

- An HTML form is used to take user input.

- Various types of inputs can be taken from a user by input tag.

- The border-style property is used for styling the HTML elements using CSS.

- The div tag is used to group multiple elements.

Summary: LET'S PACK OUR STUFF!

- HTML takes inputs from the user with forms.
- The form tag uses an input tag with various values to take user inputs.
- In an HTML form, fieldset tag is used to group form elements.
- HTML elements can be styled with different borders like solid, dotted, dashed, double, etc.
- The border-color and border-width properties of CSS are also used to style the element's borders.
- The direction property specifies the writing direction of the text on a website.
- The div tag is a container tag used to group multiple elements in HTML, and CSS properties can be applied to the div tag to style the elements.

COMPILE YOUR LOGIC

A. Multiple Choice Questions: 

1. Which input type is used to take text input in a form?
   - a. radio
   - b. checkbox
   - c. text
   - a. None of the above

2. Which tag is used to group the form tags/elements?
   - a. <legend></legend>
   - b. <fieldset></fieldset>
   - c. <group></group>
   - d. <label></label>

3. Which of the following is a container tag?
   - a. <div></div>
   - b. <form></form>
   - c. <label></label>
   - d. All of the above

4. Which of these is not a border style?
   - a. curly
   - b. dotted
   - c. dashed
   - d. double

B. Tell whether the following statements are True/False:

1. An input tag is an empty tag.

2. The label tag is used to add text in a form.

3. The default direction of text writing is right to left.

4. A div tag is a container tag.

C. Fill in the blanks:

1. _____________ is used to take user input on a website.

2. "ltr" value of direction property stands for _____________ .

3. _____________ property is used to add borders.

4. To group the HTML elements, _____________ tag is used.

D. Short Answer type Questions:

1. How to make a form in HTML?

2. What are the types of inputs in a form?

3. What are the values of direction property?

4. How to define a border width?

E. Long Answer type Questions:

1. Explain the form and grouping of form elements in HTML.
2. Explain the borders and border styling in CSS.
3. Explain the div tag with examples.
4. Explain direction property with values.

Complete the code to add a green-colored dashed border to the given heading of a website with a yellow-white colored gradient background.

Sandbox

Coding Workbench

Activity

Dark Mode   Run

```html
<html>
<head>
<style>
_______________________________________________
_______________________________________________
</style>
</head>
<body>
<center><h1><em>Play with Magic</em></h1></center>
</body>
</html>
```

Hint: Your output should look like this.

Play with Magic

Sam is the coordinator of the Children's day celebration event in his school. He wants to make a form for the school website where he can take the information of the participants with the performance details. Help Sam to create a form and add the required fields in the form.

Explore the code

Write the HTML and CSS structure to create a 'Blood Donation Camp' webpage as given below. Take the donor details using the form and add the required fields.

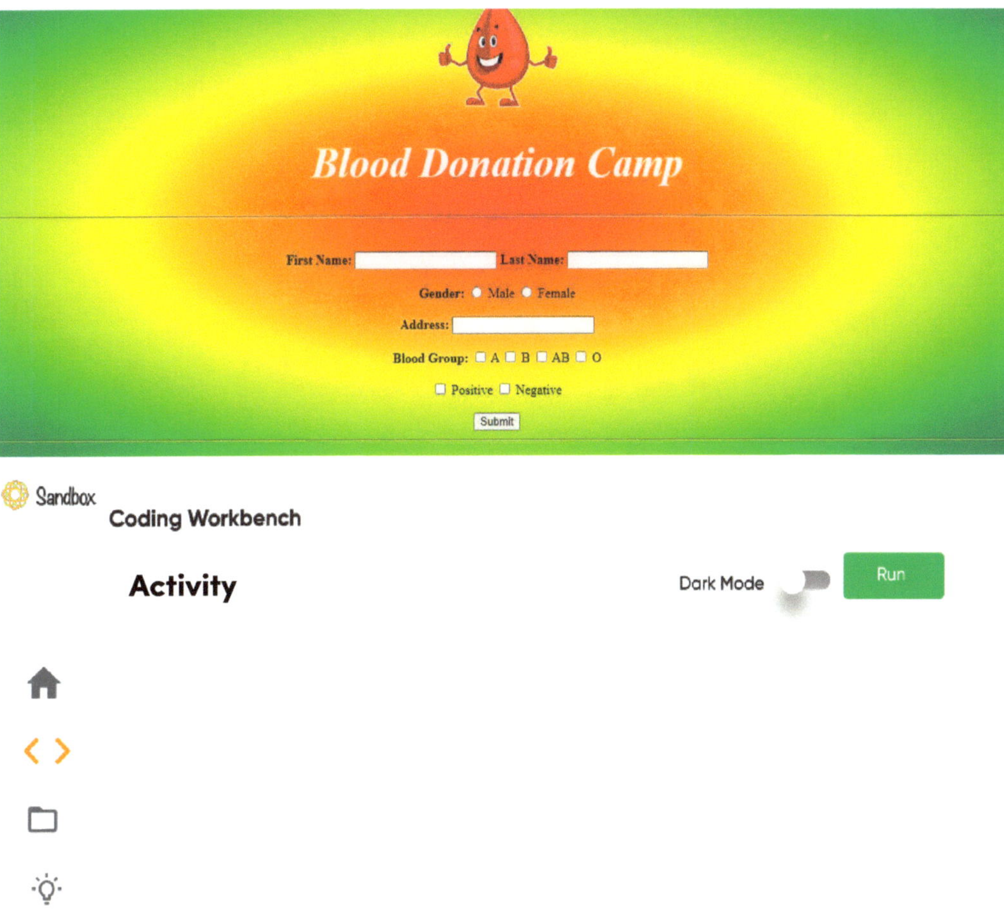

Hint: Create a form and group the form elements.
Also, use the background styling with CSS.

Sam is creating a login page for the registered members of a library. He wants to make a small form where the members can use their credentials to log in and access the benefits on the website. Add the missing statements to complete the login page.

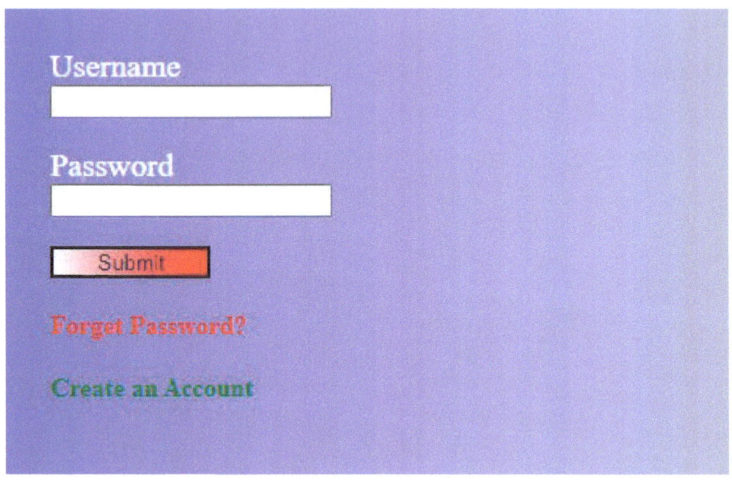

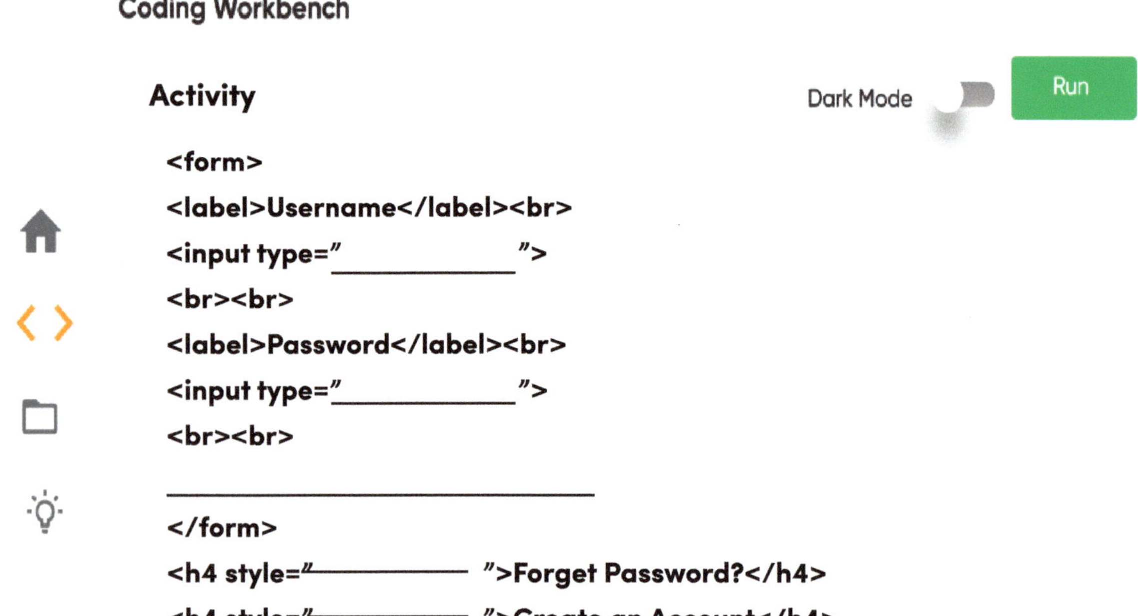

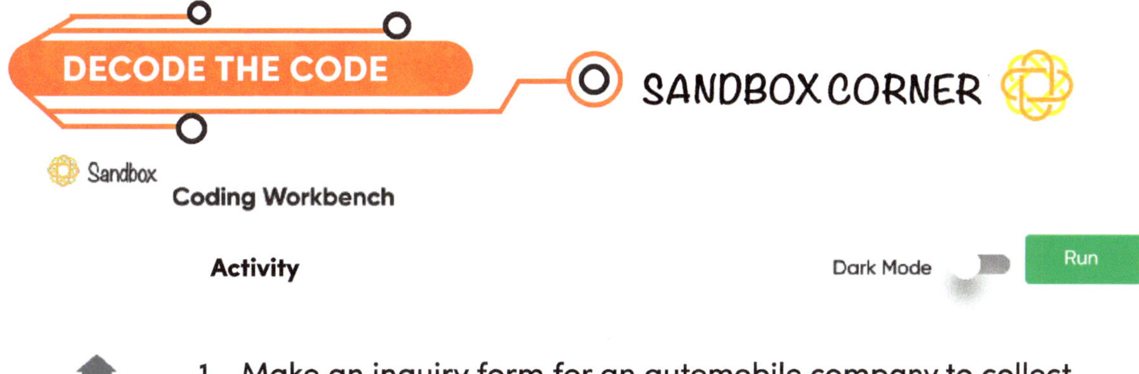

1. Make an inquiry form for an automobile company to collect customer details and capture their interest in a newly launched sports car.

2. Create a webpage to book a vocational trip. Add a form to it to take the requirements and details of the travelers.

4 DYNAMIC WEBPAGES

OVERVIEW

- Universal selector
- Background images
- Multi-Page website
- Box model
- Navigation bar

REFRESH YOUR LOGIC!

- An HTML form is used to take user input.
- Various types of inputs can be taken from a user by input tag.
- The border-style property is used for styling the HTML elements using CSS.
- The div tag is used to group multiple elements.

1. Universal selector and background image

A universal selector is used to apply a CSS property to all website elements. The universal selector is defined using the **Asterisk (*)** symbol.

For example, to change the font color of the whole website, a universal selector can be used as:

***{ color: red; }**

A background image can be added as a website background or to an element background using the CSS property, **"background-image"**.

Syntax:

```
body{
    background-image:url ("image.jpg");
}
```

Tech Fact

URL is used to address any resource on the internet as well as a file stored locally.

Here the image name with its file location or image link can be used inside the quotation marks. Also, the background image can be adjusted using its width and height
Syntax: **background-size: width(in %) height(in %);**

Let's adjust the background image of a website:

```
<html>
<head>
<title>Website with a Background</title>
<style>
*{
  color: red;
 }
body{
  background-image:url("image.jpg");
  background-size: 100% 100%;
 }
</style>
</head>
<body>
<h1>This Website has a Background</h1>
</body>
</html>
```

2. Multi-page websites

A multi-page website is created by integrating/connecting multiple web pages together. This can be done using an anchor tag, which is a container tag and requires a link or the address of another webpage.

An anchor tag is used to make a hyperlink by enclosing a piece of text, image, button, etc.

For example,

<a href = "contact.html"> Contact Us </a>

Where the **"Contact Us"** text will become a hyperlink. So, when a user clicks on it, it opens the **"contact.html"** webpage.

Let's create a multipage website by following the below steps:

Step 1: Create two HTML files in the editor with the names **index.html** and **index2.html**.

Step 2: Add the basic structure of HTML and some information in both files.

Step 3: Add an anchor tag and provide the value of href as **"index2.html".** This will create the hyperlink.

Step 4: Open the **"index.html"** file in a web browser and click on the hyperlink, it will open the "index2.html" web page. This is how a multi-Page website is created.

3. Box model

The box model is used to design the website layout using **margins, paddings, and borders.** Margins and paddings are the transparent spaces that are given outside and inside the border, respectively. Border provides outside lining (border) to the element.

Margin:

The margin CSS property is the space given outside the border of content. It can be given in pixels or percentages. Margin can be given to four different sides, i.e., top, right, bottom, and left.

Syntax:

```
div{
        margin-top: 50px;
        margin-right: 20px;
        margin-bottom: 100px;
        margin-left: 80px;
    }
```

Tech Fact

If the direction of the margin is not given then the margin is applied to all the directions.

Padding:

The padding CSS property is the space given inside the border of the content and is transparent. It can also be given in pixels and percentages with directions as top, right, bottom, and left.

Syntax:

```
div {
        padding-top: 50px;
        padding-right: 20px;
        padding-bottom: 100px;
        padding-left: 80px;
    }
```

Let's change the layout of a website using the box model.

Step 1: Create a webpage with some text and image information.

```
<center><h1><i>Force and Pressure</i></h1></center>
<p><strong>Gravitational force:</strong> the attractive force of earth which
acts upon all the objects is called the force of gravity or gravitational force.</p>
<p><b>Pressure:</b> The force acting on a unit area of a surface is called
pressure.</p>
<img src="https://o.quizlet.com/o9nilUpTP3GBtfON-DFZIQ.png" width="250px">
```

Step 2: Group the elements and apply styling with colors and borders.

```
<style>
  body{
    background-color: orange;
      }
  h1{
     color: purple;
      }
  div{
    color: red;
    background-image:
    radial-gradient(purple, white, pink);
    border-style: solid;
    border-color: purple;
      }
</style>
```

Step 3: Change the layout of the content using margins and paddings.

```css
div{
        color: red;
        background-image: radial-gradient(purple, white, pink);
        border-style: solid;
        border-color: purple;
        padding-right: 50px;
        padding-left: 50px;
        margin-left: 50px;
        margin-right: 50px;
}
```

Step 4: Your output will look like as given below:

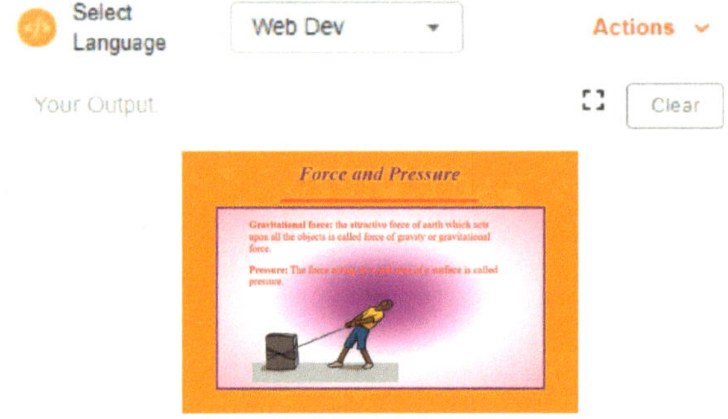

4. Navigation bar

The navigation bar or nav bar is used to create a menu for a website. It shows how many features or different web pages are linked to the website. Using some CSS properties, the nav bar can be designed vertically or horizontally. Navigation bar elements are enclosed and grouped with a nav tag.

Let's create a navigation bar for a website.

Step 1: Create an unordered list of navbar options in a nav bar tag.

```html
<nav>
    <ul>
    <li>Home</li>
    <li>About</li>
    <li>Newsletter</li>
    <li>Locate Us</li>
    </ul>
</nav>
```

Tech Fact

An anchor tag is used with all the items of a nav bar to make it a hyperlink.

Step 2: Add the CSS properties with nav tag and list items.

```
<style>
    nav {
      background-color: #1f276e;
      padding: 5px;
    }
    li {
      list-style-type: none;
      display: inline;
      padding: 10px;
      color: white;
    }
</style>
```

Step 3: Add styling of the nav bar using background color and hover effect.

```
 li:hover {
      background-color: white;
      color: #1f276e;
    }
```

Step 4: The navigation bar looks like this:

REFRESH YOUR LOGIC!

- The universal selector adds CSS property to all website elements.
- Multiple web pages can be grouped to create a website using an anchor tag.
- Margins and paddings are used to change the layout of a website.

DID YOU KNOW

Windows Notepad is a simple text editor for Windows; it creates and edits plain text documents. It was first released in 1983 to commercialize the computer mouse in MS-DOS.

COMPILE YOUR LOGIC

A. Multiple Choice Questions: 

1. What is the symbol of a universal selector?

    a. /
    b. *
    c. +
    d. -

2. What is the full form of "URL"?

    a. Universal Resource Locator
    b. Universal Resource Location
    c. Uniform Resource Locator
    d. United Resource Locator

3. What is the full form of "href"?

    a. hypertext reference
    b. height text reference
    c. highlight reference
    d. All of the above

4. Which of the following is used to change the layout of the website?

    a. Box Size
    b. Box Space
    c. Box Color
    d. Box Model

B. Tell whether the following statements are True/False:

1. Multi-Page websites can be created without hyperlinks. ☐

2. A navigation bar displays the main content of a website. ☐

3. An unordered list is used to add navbar options. ☐

4. Margin cannot be applied to images. ☐

C. Fill in the blanks:

1. The space given inside the border is ____________ .

2. ______________ displays the menu of a website.

3. A universal selector is defined with the ________________ symbol.

4. The ________________ property is used to adjust the background image.

D. Short Answer type Questions:

1. What is a universal selector?

2. How to add a website's background image?

3. Which tag is used to link multiple web pages?

4. How to give margins to all four directions?

E. Long Answer type Questions:

1. Explain the box model.
2. How to create a multipage website? Explain step by step.
3. Explain the universal selector with examples.
4. How to create a navigation bar? Explain with examples.

The given webpage has to be connected to the homepage of the website. The name of the homepage HTML file is "index.html" and is located at the same location. Complete the code and connect both files.

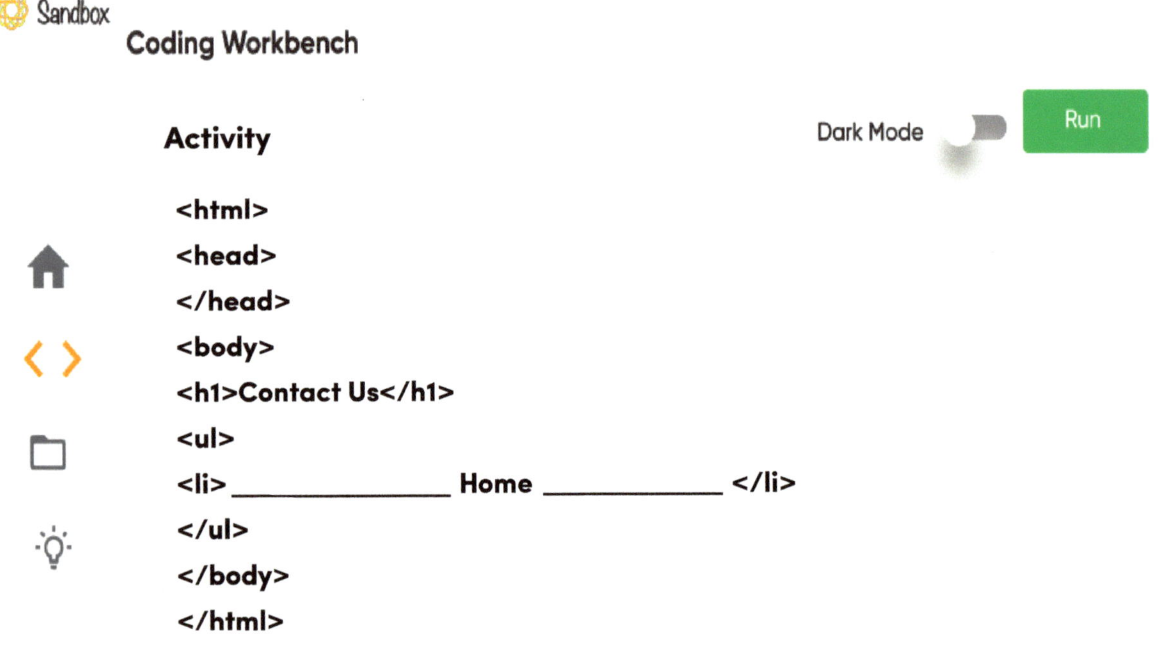

Hint: Use the anchor tag with the hypertext reference of the homepage.

Sam wants to make a homepage for an energy-drink-selling company. He wants to display all the services and products provided by the company. Help Sam create a homepage using a navigation bar and a good information layout.

Explore the code

Create a webpage on GOOGLE search where the navigation bar displays Google services like Gmail, Classroom, etc., and adjust the layout as shown below.

Hint: Use images for the logo and search bar.

Understand the code better

Sam wants to create a website for a dirt bike race that would be held next month. He has all the information about the event which he wants to display on the website. But he creating the website, he forgot to add and adjust the background image. Complete the code and help Sam add and adjust the background on the website.

Sandbox

Coding Workbench

Activity

Dark Mode | Run

```html
<html>
<head>
<title>Dirt Bike Tournament</title>
<style>_________________________________
       _________________________________
       _________________________________
</style>
</head>
<body>...</body>
</html>
```

Hint: Use the image location or link with the CSS property.

DECODE THE CODE — SANDBOX CORNER

Sandbox

Coding Workbench

Activity

Dark Mode | Run

1. Create your portfolio website with text and image information like personal details, educational details, sports details, hobbies, and achievements.

2. Create a website on "Save Water" to display the need for saving water, do's and dont's while using water, etc. Add a background to the website.

Master Worksheet – Section 2

Master Your Logic 

A. Fill in the blanks

1. The universal selector is defined using the _______________ symbol.

2. _______________ CSS property is used to add background images.

3. <a> tag stands for _______________ .

4. Margins and Paddings can be given in _______________ directions.

5. _______________ input type creates a submit button in an HTML form.

B. Match the columns

Column A	Column B
1. Class Attribute	A. Types of borders applied using CSS.
2. <input type = "radio">	B. The default text direction is from right to left.
3. dotted, solid, dashed	C. It is a container tag for an HTML document
4. rtl	D. It provides a unique identity to an element
5. Div Tag	E. It creates a radio button for choosing an option.

Activity:
A website on the telescope is given below where the information is added using paragraphs and heading. From the options given below pick up the CSS properties and write them in the box which can achieve the paragraphs styling as given below:-

TELESCOPE

A telescope is a device used to observe distant objects by their emission, absorption, or reflection of electromagnetic radiation.

The first telescopes were created in the Netherlands in 1608.

I. .first { color: yellow }
II. .second { color: white; }
III. p { color: yellow, white; }
IV. p { color: yellow-white; }

Write the CSS for paragraphs here

SCHOOL ESSENTIALS

a. font-size: 30px;
b. background-color: white;
c. border-style: dashed;
d. border-width: 5px;

Write the CSS for paragraphs here

# Challenge Your Logic

Activity:
An NGO in the country needs a form that can be added to the website to take inquiries from the people. Write down the missing HTML code for the form to get the desired output. The output should look like this

Need Help?

Enter Your Name

Contact Nos

Address

Animal Type?

☐ **Cat** ☐ **Dog Other**

Submit | Reset

```
<html>
<head><title>NGO</title></head>
<body>
<form>
<fieldset>
<legend>_____________________ </legend>
<label>Enter Your Name</label>
<input_______________ >

_______________________________________
_______________________________________
_______________________________________
_______________________________________
_______________________________________
_______________________________________

<input type="reset">
</fieldset>
</form>
</body>
</html>
```

Activity:

Create a navigation bar for a Lotus webpage as given below. Consider that the navigation bar options are already added with the HTML elements. Write the CSS properties and their values applied to the elements.

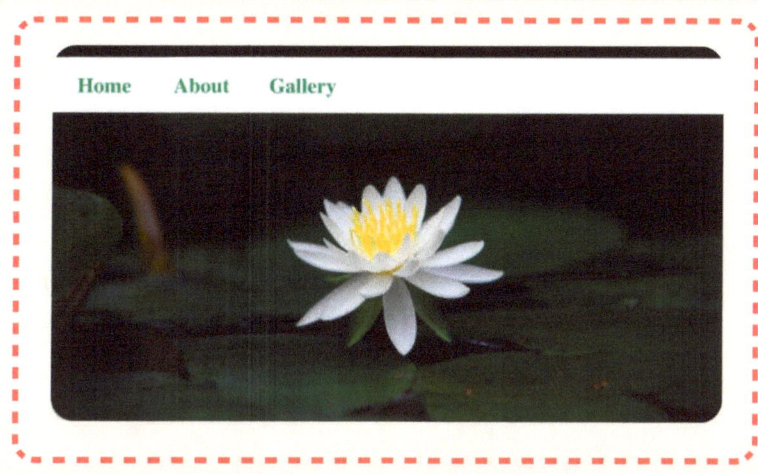

Write the CSS for paragraphs here

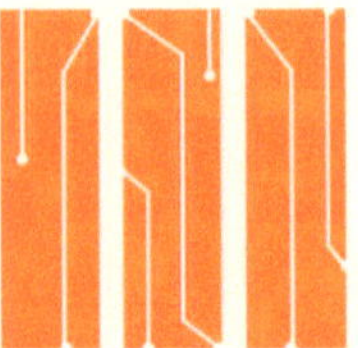

ALGORITHMS & PROGRAMMING

This section deep dives into the coding and programming world. Kids get introduced to algorithmic thinking, concepts of programming and writing programs using block-based programming (Scratch) and text-based programming (Python)

OVERVIEW

* Conditionals
* Logical operators
* Loops: For & While loops
* Nested loops
* Empty loop theory
* Loops with conditionals

REFRESH YOUR LOGIC!

* Variables can be used to store an alphanumeric value in a program.
* Data types define the type of value a variable can hold.
* A list can contain multiple values of different data types.
* To call a function, it has to be defined first.

1. Conditional statements

Conditional statements allow you to run specific instructions when a given condition becomes true.

Let's create a condition for crossing a road:

```
traffic_light = "red"
if traffic_light == "red":
        print ("Cross the Road")
```

The above example prints "Cross the Road" only when the traffic light for the cars becomes red.

Complete the following flowchart to check if the entered letter is a vowel or not and print the required output.

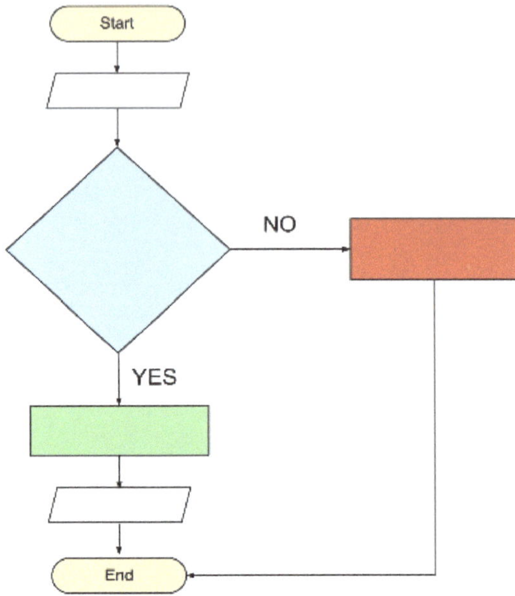

2. Logical operators

Logical operators are used to build decision-making capability by connecting two or more expressions. Commonly used logical operators are **AND, OR and NOT.**

2.1 AND operator

Logical **"AND"** operator is used to check if all the given conditions are true. If any of the given conditions is not true, then it will return false.

e.g, if there are two levels of test and you pass the test when level 1 **AND** level 2 are cleared. You would only pass the test when both levels are cleared. The result will be fail of only one level is cleared.

2.2 OR operator

Logical **"OR"** operator is used to check if even one of the given conditions is true. If any condition is true, it returns true. Only if all the conditions are false, it returns false.

e.g, if you were told by the doctor to walk 5kms daily, you can decide to go for an evening **OR** a morning walk. Here, if you take either a morning walk or evening walk, you complete your daily walking requirement. Only when you do not go for both

2.3 NOT operator

Logical **"NOT"** is used to check the reverse of a condition. If the condition is true, it returns false. If the condition is not true, then it returns true.

3. Understanding If-Else and Else-if

3.1 If-Else condition

If-Else statement is used in a program when two different sets of instructions are executed based on the result of a condition. If the condition is true, then the particular set of instructions are executed, else if the condition is not true, then the instruction defined under 'else' are executed.

Let's create an If-Else condition:

```
Num = int (input ("Enter a Number:"))
If Num%2==1:
                print ("The number is Odd")
else:
                print ("The number is Even")
```

3.2 Else-if condition

Else-if statement is used along with an If statement. When a program needs to check more than one conditions to run a specific set of instructions, then else-if is used.

In python else-if is written as "elif". Let's create an else-if statement to see its usage:

```
Num = int (input ("Enter a Number:"))
If Num>0:
                print ("The number is Positive")
elif Num<0:
                print ("The number is Negative")
else:
                print ("The number is Zero")
```

4. Recap of loops

Loops are used in a program to continuosly repeat a set of instructions in the program for a known number of repetition or until a given condition is met. It reduces code length and increases the performance of the program.

There are two different types of loops:

- **FOR Loop**
- **WHILE Loop**

4.1 FOR loop

The FOR loop is used to iterate over a sequence. It uses a variable that counts the number of iterations and has a fixed known number of repititions/iterations.

4.2 WHILE loop

The WHILE loop keeps repeating the set of instructions until the given condition is met. Before executing the loop, the loop tests whether the given condition has been met or not. The number of iterations are indefinite and completely decided by the condition.

4.3 Nested loop

A loop inside a loop is known as a nested loop. The inner loop works in the range of the outer loop.

For example, If two lists are given – one for the toppings and another for the bases of a pizza and the desired output of the program is to get all the combinations of possible toppings with all possible bases, then the following would be the program:

```
toppings = ["Onion", "Tomato", "Capsicum"]
Base = ["Pan Crust", "Thin Crust", "Cheese Burst"]
for i in toppings:
        for j in Base:
                print(i, j)
```

Output:
Onion Pan Crust
Onion Thin Crust
Onion Cheese Burst
Tomato Pan Crust
Tomato Thin Crust
Tomato Cheese Burst
Capsicum Pan Crust
Capsicum Thin Crust
Capsicum Cheese Burst

5. Difference between FOR and WHILE loop

FOR Loop	WHILE Loop
• It is used when the number of iterations is known. It is also known as a definite loop.	• It is used when the number of iterations is unknown.
• It has a counter variable initialized in the declaration.	• It doesn't have a built-in loop control variable.
• When we know how many times a set of instructions has to be repeated, then FOR loop is preferred.	• When we want to repeat a set of instructions until a given condition is met, then a WHILE loop is preferred.

6. Examples of FOR loop

Example 1

Let's find the factorial of a number using for loop and conditionals. Conditionals are used to check if the entered number is positive or not.

FACTORIAL: The product of all positive integers less than or equal to a given positive integer. E.g.the factorial of 5 would be calculated as follows:

5x4x3x2x1 or 1x2x3x4x5, or 120

Complete the program by adding the required conditionals:

```python
print("Find the Factorial of a Number")
num = int(input( ______________ ))
factorial = 1
if ________ :
    print("Sorry, factorial does not exist for negative number")
elif num == 0:
        print(" __________________ ")
else:
        for i in range(1,num + 1):
        factorial = factorial*i
print( __________________ )
```

where **range ()** function stores the minimum and maximum values of the loop variable as **range (minimum value, maximum value).**

Example 2

Sam has to find out the factors of a number. The program checks if the number entered by Sam is perfectly divisible with any of the numbers between 1 to the entered number.

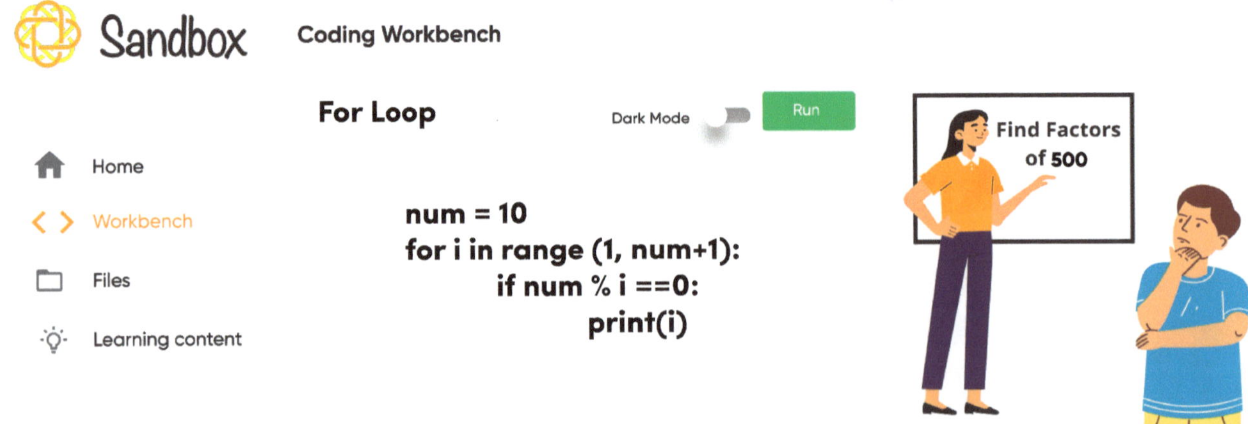

Here, num is a variable with an integer value as 10. The loop checks if 10 is perfectly divisible by any numbers between 1 to 10 and prints those numbers.

7. Examples of WHILE loop

Example 1

Let's calculate the sum of "n" natural numbers. The user provides input for "n" and the while loop should add the numbers until "n" is reached.

```
n =________ (input("Enter the Number: ")___
sum = 0
i = 1
while __________:
        sum = sum + i
        i = i+1
print ("The sum is", sum)
```

Example 2

Sam saw a pattern of stars on a wall while coming back home from his school and he decides to draw the same pattern of stars using a program. So, he writes an algorithm as given below:

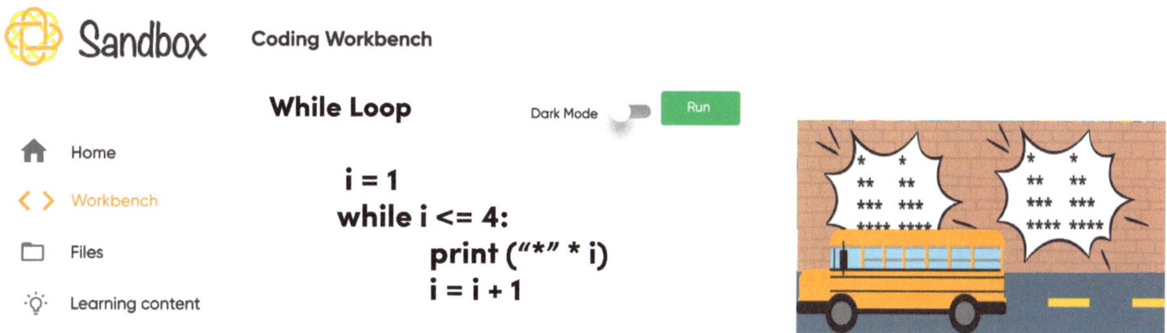

where i is the variable starting from 1 and going up to 4 using the while loop. After drawing one star, the value of i increases by 1 and it draws two stars. This process continues until i becomes 4 as the while loop keeps on repeating the logic until the condition of i<=4 is not true anymore.

8. Empty loop theory

Empty loop is a loop with no instructions inside it to repeat. It is used to pass the program to the next command even if the condition of the loop becomes true.

In an empty loop, we use the **"pass"** keyword which does nothing and moves to the next statement of the program.

For example,

```
Season = "Summer"t
While (Season == "Summer"):
        pass
print ("Empty Loop Passed")
```

where **"Season"** is the variable with value as **"Summer"**. While loop checks the condition and since it is true, it passes the program to the next statement and gives the output as **"Empty Loop Passed".**

9. Applying loops with conditionals

Loops can be used along with conditional statements. Based on the program's requirements, we can select one of the two loops – FOR or WHILE.

Let's find the sum of all the even numbers between 1 and the number as entered by the user. Complete the program by providing the required statements.

Tech Fact

Empty function can also be created same as empty loop

```
num = int( _______________ )
Sum = 0
for i in range (1, num+1):
    if ( ____________ ):
        Sum = Sum + i
print(_________)
```

REFRESH YOUR LOGIC!

- An empty loop is used to pass the program.
- Loops can be applied with conditionals in a program.
- Multiple conditionals can be added using else-if.
- Nested conditionals can be created within the loops as well.

Summary: LET'S PACK OUR STUFF!

- Conditional statements run the code when the condition is true.
- If-else and else-if are used as conditional statements.
- Else-if can be used when multiple conditions are required to be checked.
- Loops are used to repeat a set of instructions.
- FOR loop can repeat for a specific range of values.
- WHILE loop repeats until the given condition continue to be true or becomes true.
- An empty loop is used to pass the program.

DID YOU KNOW

Python was conceived in the late 1980s by Guido van Rossum at Centrum Wiskunde & Informatica (CWI) in the Netherlands.

COMPILE YOUR LOGIC

A. Multiple Choice Questions:

1. Which loop has a counter variable in its declaration?
   - a. For
   - b. While
   - c. Nested
   - d. None

2. A loop inside a loop is known as
   - a. For loop
   - b. While loop
   - c. Nested loop
   - d. Empty loop

3. Which conditional statement has only one condition?
   - a. If
   - b. If-else
   - c. Else-if
   - d. a and b both

4. Which command is used to make an empty loop?
   - a. empty
   - b. pass
   - c. break
   - d. Continue

B. Tell whether the following statements are True/False:

1. An Empty loop can hold various statements.

2. Loops can be used with nested conditionals.

3. A variable cannot be declared inside a loop.

4. A while loop repeats the logic until the condition becomes true.

C. Fill in the blanks:

1. A loop inside a loop is _______________ loop.

2. A while loop runs until the condition becomes _______________ .

3. The range keyword is used in _______________ loop.

4. _______________ statement is used in the Empty loop to move the program.

D. Short Answer type Questions:

1. What is a loop?

2. What is an empty loop?

3. What is a nested Loop?

4. Give an advantage of using a loop.

E. Long Answer type Questions:

1. Explain the FOR loop with an example.

2. Explain the difference between the FOR and WHILE loops.

3. Briefly explain If-Else and Else-if.

4. Explain loops with conditionals with examples.

Solve the code together

Fill up the water cycle process in a proper sequence and show how these processes repeat in a loop in the nature.

Hint: Check the science notebook for your reference

ACTIVITY:

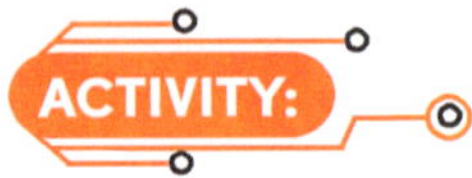

Sam wants to set the alarm for his music classes that would happen once a week, i.e., on Wednesday at 5 pm. Create a program to buzz the alarm every week at the required time

Explore the code

Write down the tasks in a step-by-step manner that repeat every day in your daily life routine.

Hint: Consider your morning-evening routine, playing time, study time, etc.

Sam wants to draw a flowchart presentation to describe the functionality of a WHILE loop (the loop keeps repeating the statement until the condition becomes true). Use the below space to complete the flowchart.

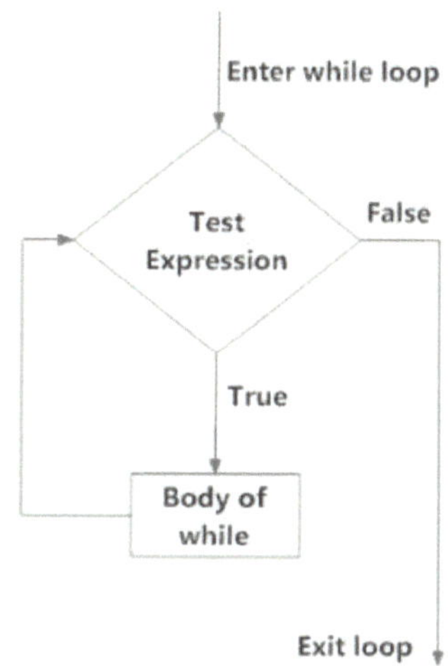

DECODE THE CODE

SANDBOX CORNER

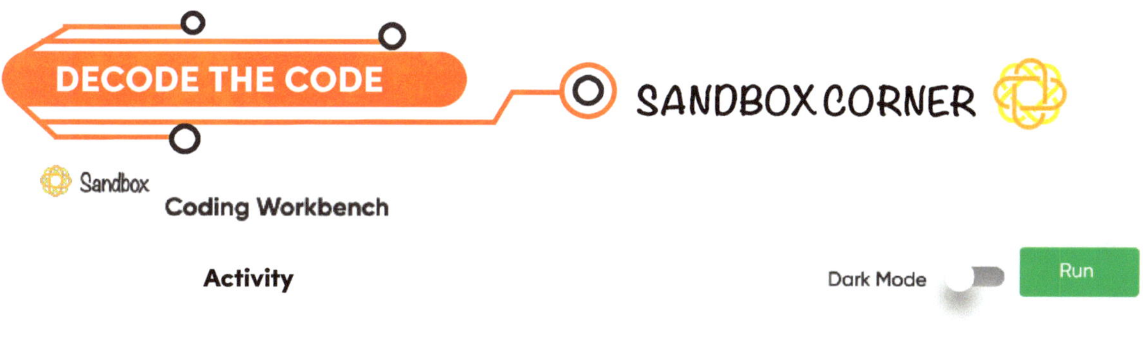

Sandbox

Coding Workbench

Activity

Dark Mode   Run

1. Write a program to check if an alphabet is a vowel or not. Use loops with conditionals.

2. Write a program to print the squares of all the even numbers between 1 to 15 using loops with conditions.

OVERVIEW

- Functions
- Function parameters
- Return values from a function
- Applications of functions

REFRESH YOUR LOGIC!

- Conditional statements run a set of instructions when a given condition is true.
- Loops are used to repeat a task and reduce the length of code.
- FOR loop is used when the number of iterations are known.
- WHILE loop keeps repeating the command until the given condition becomes true.

1. Function recap

A function is a piece of code that can be used multiple times in a program, thereby eliminiating the need for writing it fully every time. The **"def"** keyword is used to define a function.

Syntax of function:

def function_name(parameter):
    function's statements/instructions
    print/return statement

Let's define and call a function using block-based programming:

Tech Fact

Function & variables follow the same naming rules.

Step 1: Open Scratch Editor, add a sprite of a ball, and a glass with a backdrop as shown:

Step 2: Add the blocks to move the ball on the screen. Whenever the ball touches the glass, call a function to start a glass breaking sound.

Fig 6.1

Fig 6.2

ACTIVITY:

Complete the following code to find out the area of a cube when value of one side of the cube is given by the user. Define and call the function.

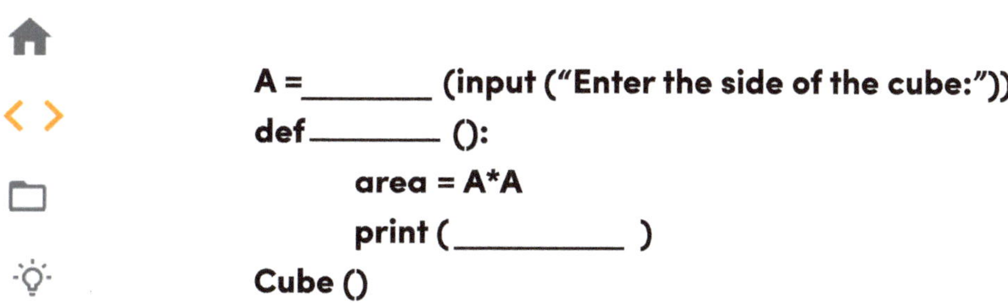

2. Function parameters

Function parameters act as variables inside the function. Parameters are specified inside the parentheses of the function.

def counter(a,b):

where **a & b** are parameters of the function **counter.**

When the function is called, a value is given as an argument to assign it to the parameter of the function for further use inside the function.

Let's create a function with parameters to find out the perimeter of a rectangle:

Sandbox

Coding Workbench

Activity

Dark Mode   Run

```
A = int (input ("Enter Length:"))
B = int (input ("Enter Breadth:"))
def perimeter (L, B):
    peri =————————————————
    print (————————————————  )
————————— (A, B)
```

REFRESH YOUR LOGIC!

- Function executes a set of instructions to perform a specific task.
- Function parameter works as an input variable.

3. Returning values from a function

A function returns the calculated value or the output by using the **"return"** keyword. The **return** keyword finishes the execution of a function and returns a value from a function.

Let's create a function that returns the volume of the cuboid:

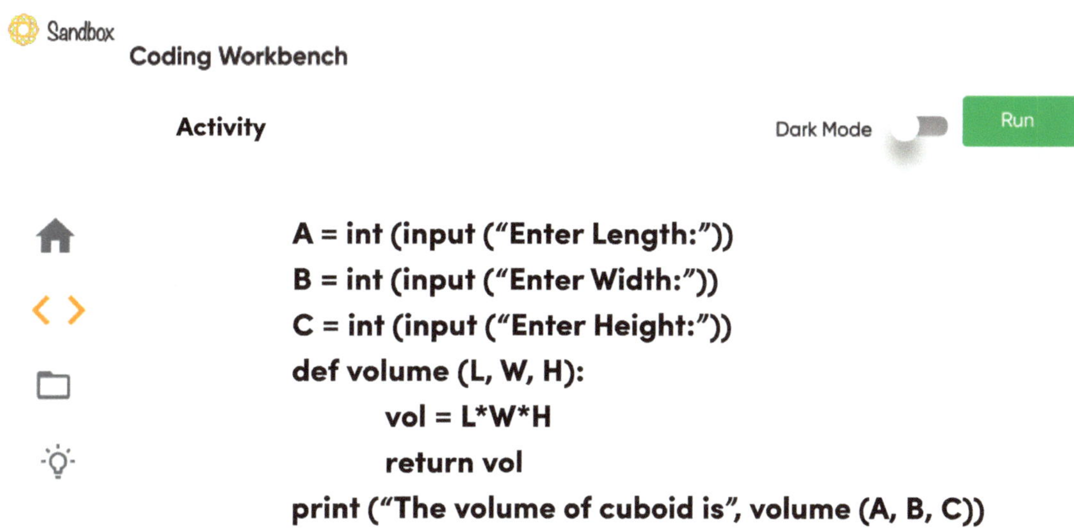

ACTIVITY:

Create the same function with parameters to find out the volume of a cuboid in the SCRATCH editor and write down the steps below.

____

____

____

____

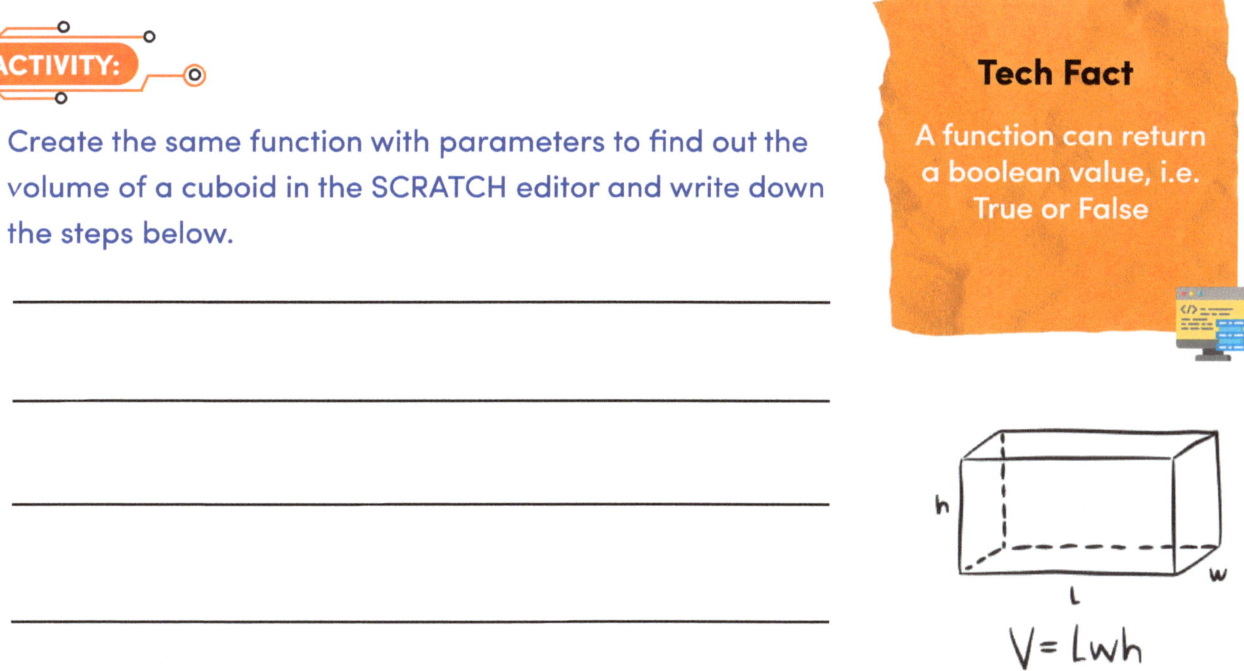

Tech Fact

A function can return a boolean value, i.e. True or False

4. How to reduce redundancy using functions?

Redundancy means the repetition of something unnecessary. Hence, if we have a set of instructions in a program are repeated multiple times, it increases redundancy. Redundancy can be reduced by creating and using functions in the program wherever repetitions occur.

Let's understand this with an example of making a sandwich. To make a sandwich, we need to follow a few steps:

Step 1: Take bread, butter and jam.

Step 2: Slice the bread.

Step 3: Spread jam and butter.

Step 4: Combine the slices.

These 4 steps must be followed to make a sandwich. These need to be repeated every time we make a sandwich. However, instead of repeating these 4 steps again and again, we can define a function as **"Make a Sandwich",** to combine all the 4 steps in a single command. Hence, a function can remove redundancy by reducing the repetition of the instructions in the program and thereby minimizing errors.

5. Applications of functions

Treadmill in Gym: The most common machine used in the gym follows a set of instructions to move the conveyor belt forward and backward. The machine has some in-built functions and responds based on which ones are called by the user.

Washing Machine: The washing machine has some in-built functions like washing clothes, drying the clothes, etc. which the operator can call.

Weather prediction: The prediction of weather involves calculation of ongoing temperature with wind speed and amount of cloud cover. This calculation uses functions with parameters.

REFRESH YOUR LOGIC!

- Return value is also an output of a function.
- Functions can be used everywhere in real life to execute a specific task.

Summary: LET'S PACK OUR STUFF!

- Functions are a set of instructions that can be called after defining.
- Functions can take inputs as parameters.
- The value given while calling a function is called an argument, that is assigned to a parameter.
- Functions can give output as a return value.

DID YOU KNOW

The role of the coding and marking industry in food safety is identical to providing the right packaging material for a specific food type for food protection.

COMPILE YOUR LOGIC

A. Multiple Choice Questions:

1. Rules for naming a function are similar to

    a. Conditions
    b. Loops
    c. Variable
    d. None of the above

2. Which of the following is used to call a function?

    a. Function Return value
    b. Function Argument
    c. Function Parameter
    d. Function Name

3. Where can we use the arguments?

    a. Conditions
    b. Loops
    c. Functions
    d. None of the above

4. Which command is used to make an empty loop?

    a. Argument
    b. Return
    c. Loop
    d. All of the above

B. Tell whether the following statements are True/False:

1. Functions cannot return a value.

2. Functions are the same as loops.

3. A function reduces the length of the code.

4. A function can be used with conditionals..

C. Fill in the blanks:

1. Returned value is also known as ____________ of a function.

2. ______________ are used to reduce the lines of code.

3. A variable that takes input for a function is ______________ .

4. Function executes a ______________ of instructions.

1. What is a function?

2. How to define a function?

3. How to call a function?

4. What are the parameters and arguments of a function?

1. Explain how to define and call a function.
2. What are parameters in a function? Explain with examples.
3. Briefly explain the return value of a function.
4. Briefly explain the advantages of using functions.

STEP UP YOUR CODE GAME

Complete the following blank commands in the program to check the working performance of a refrigerator.

The refrigerator is to be rated as per the following:

- Excellent – if the rating is above 7
- Mediocre – if the rating is between 4 and 7 (both 4 and 7 included)
- Poor – if the rating if below 4

# Sandbox   Coding Workbench

Activity   Dark Mode   Run

- Home
- Workbench
- Files
- Learning content

```
Rating = int(input("Rate out of 10: "))
def perform:
        if Rating>7:
                print("Excellent Performance")
        elif________:
                print("_______________")
        else:
                print("_____________")
perform()
```

**Hint: From 0 to 3 ratings, the performance will be "Poor"
and from 4 to 7 ratings, the performance will be "Average".**

Sam wants to create a program that checks the weather. If it's too hot, then he should get an umbrella along with him while going out and if it's not too hot, then he can go without an umbrella. Help him build the program.

Create a sequence of blocks in the Scratch editor to calculate the square root of a number. Take the number as an input parameter to a function, calculate the square root and print it over the screen.

Hint: Use the backdrop of the classroom and sprites of teacher and student.

A farmer wants to calculate the profit percentage earned in the last year by using the amount of money he spent and the amount of money he received by selling the harvest.

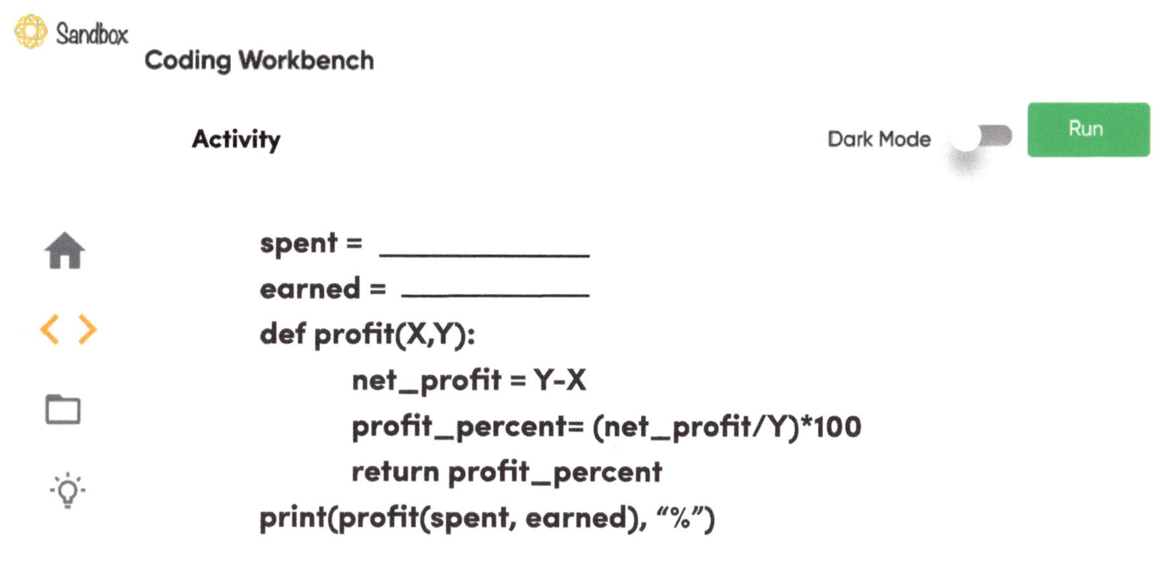


```
spent = ______________
earned = ______________
def profit(X,Y):
        net_profit = Y-X
        profit_percent= (net_profit/Y)*100
        return profit_percent
print(profit(spent, earned), "%")
```

Hint: Take the spent and earned as input and create a function.

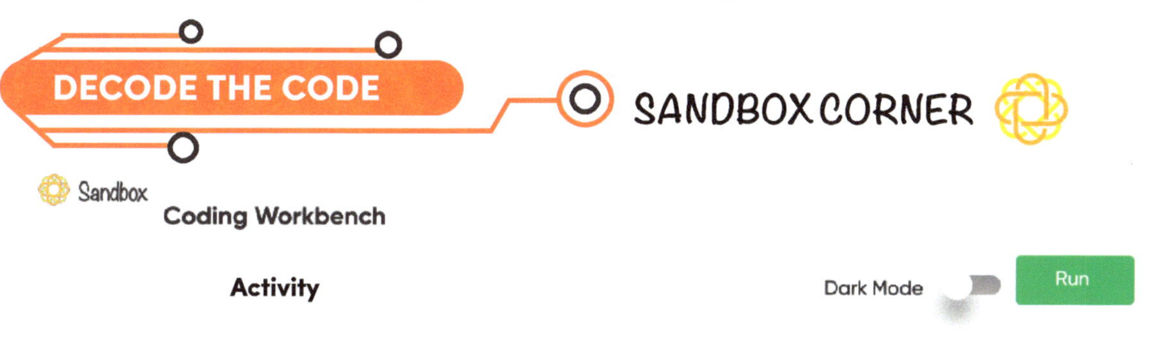

1. A famous clothing store in the city makes a report at the end of the day about the available stock (in percentage) in the store. Create a function to calculate the available stock and print the report.

2. Create a sequence of blocks in the Scratch editor to calculate the area of the circle where the radius is given by the user.

7 PROGRAMMING WITH ARRAYS

OVERVIEW

- Array and its sorting
- Lists and Tuples
- Difference between a List and a Tuple
- Data modification in List and Tuples

REFRESH YOUR LOGIC!

- Functions are used to run a set of instructions to perform a specific task.
- Variables and functions follow the same naming rules.
- A nested loop is when a loop runs inside another loop.
- Common logical operators used are AND, OR and NOT.

1. Array recap

An array is a variable that can store multiple values of the same data type. An array cannot store values with different data types, all the values should be of the same data type.

Values inside the array are known as **items**. Each item in an array has a specific address, known as the **index value.**

The 'list' data type in python is similar to an array although unlike an array, it can store values with different data types.

Tech Fact

An array is defined using square braces, i.e., []

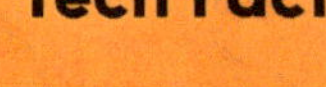

Let's understand this with the school library as an example, where all the books are arranged in a particular order so that the librarian can easily find a book in its position in the library.

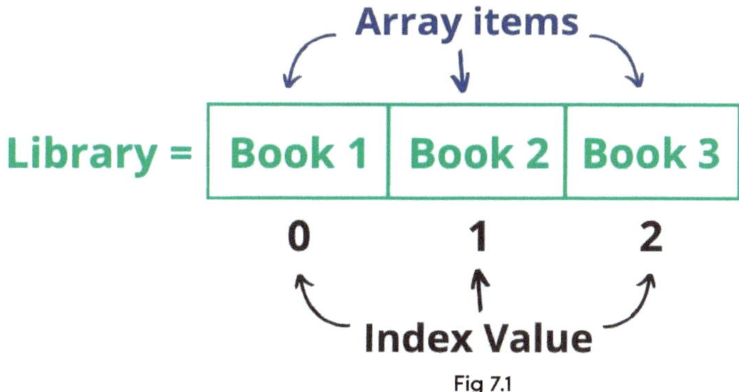

Fig 7.1

Here, Library is an array with items Book 1, Book 2, and Book 3 with index values 0, 1, and 2 respectively.

2. Sorting an array

If an array has values that are not arranged in order, then sorting helps us arrange the items in the array in either ascending or descending order.

sort () is a pre-defined function used to sort an array, by default it arranges the values or items in the ascending order. **sort()** function has a parameter named **"reverse"** with two values - True & False to decide the order type (ascending/descending).
To arrange in ascending order reverse parameter is set as false (or skipped) and for descending order, it is set as true.
variable.sort() for ascending order sort ; **variable.sort(reverse=True)** for descending.
The predefined function of **sort()** is used along with the variable.

e.g., Let's sort an array in descending and ascending order using the sort() function:

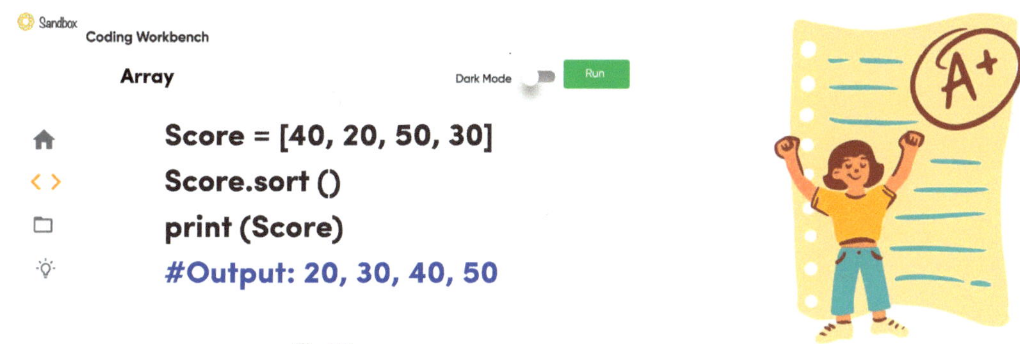

Fig 7.2

NOTE: Python uses a list as an array that can store the values with different data types and can be modified later in the program.

3. Tuples

A tuple is an ordered collection that cannot be changed once created. It is a sequence data type that stores values of any data type, similar to a list.

It uses round brackets i.e. () to store the values.

Let's create a tuple:

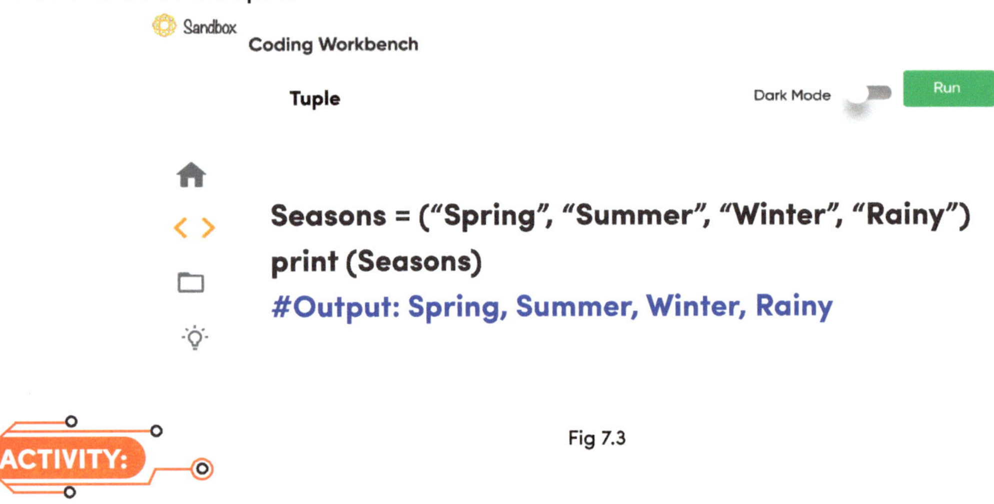

Fig 7.3

ACTIVITY:

Create a list of your favorite superheroes, create a tuple of their real-life names, and print the output.

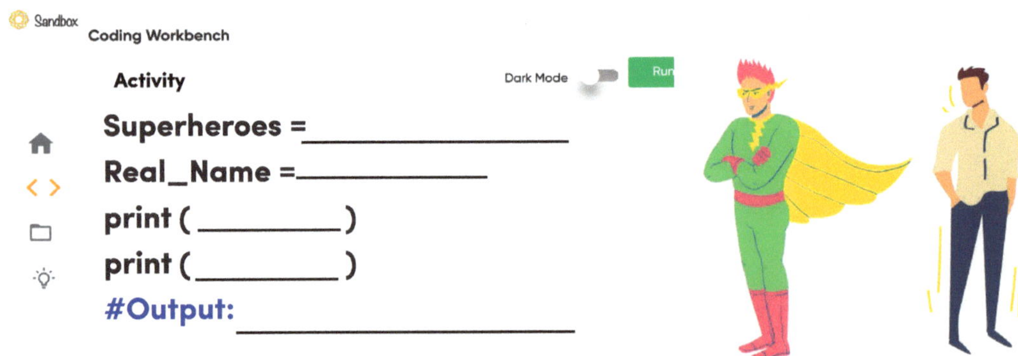

List	**Tuple**
• It is used to store data. • It can store values of different data types. • It is created using square brackets. • It can be modified later in the program. • Items can be accessed with the index value.	• It is used to store data. • It can store values of different data types. • It is created using round brackets. • It cannot be modified later in the program. • Items can be accessed with the index value.

5. Data modification in Lists and Tuples

As tuples are unchangeable, they cannot be modified once they are created, but we can access the items in a tuple with an index value.

Data modifications like **add, change, and remove** an item can be done only with the lists in python.

5.1 Access list items

We can access any list item in a list with its index value.
Let's access an item in a list:

```
Balls = ["Basketball", "Football", "Volleyball", "Cricket ball"]
print (Balls [0])
print (Balls [-1])
#Output: Basketball
          Cricket ball
```

Fig 7.4

Tech Fact

The first item in an array will always have 0 index value.

Here, Balls is a list, whose items can be accessed with its index value.

The [-1] index value refers to the last item in a list whereas the [0] index value refers to the first item in a list.

5.2 Add a list item

To add an item to a list later in the program, an append() function is used which is a built-in function in python.

Let's add an item to a list:

```
Animals = ["Mammals", "Birds", "Reptiles"]
Animals.append("Amphibians")
print (Animals)


#Output: Mammals, Birds, Reptiles, Amphibians
```

Fig 7.5

Here, append () is used to add a new item to the list. The new item is added after the last item on the list.

We can also add an item to a specific index value using the insert () function, a built-in function in python.

```
Animals = ["Mammals", "Birds", "Reptiles"]
Animals.insert(0, "Amphibians")
print (Animals)


#Output: Amphibians, Mammals, Birds
```

Fig 7.6

5.3 Change an item

We can change a list item by addressing its index value with a new item. Let's change an item in a list of Flowers:

```
Flowers = ["Rose", "Tulip", "Lotus"]
Flowers [1] = "Marigold"
print (Flowers)


#Output: Rose, Marigold, Lotus
```

Fig 7.7

When we change the list item, the previous item is replaced with a new item and occupies that index value.

5.4 Remove an item

To remove an item from a list, the built-in remove () function is used in python.

Let's remove an item from a list:

```
Mammals = ["Cats", "Dogs", "Deer"]
Mammals.remove ("Dogs")
print (Mammals)


#Output: Cats, Deer
```

Fig 7.8

Here, Mammals is the list from which an item is removed using the remove () function. We can also remove an item with its index value using the pop () function. By default, the pop () function removes the last item from a list.

For example –

```
Mammals = ["Cats", "Dogs", "Deer"]
Mammals.pop (2)
print (Mammals)


#Output: Cats, Dogs
```

Fig 7.9

REFRESH YOUR LOGIC!

- A tuple cannot be changed once it is created.
- A list and a tuple are examples of sequence data types in python.
- A list can be modified by adding, removing, or changing items in the list.

Summary: LET'S PACK OUR STUFF!

- An array can store values with similar data types.
- An array can be ordered in ascending order with the sort function.
- List and Tuples are used to store data with different or similar data types.
- Data modification can be done only with the list, as tuples are unchangeable once created.

DID YOU KNOW

E-Libraries use multiple lists of book categories to store the information of each book with its address.

COMPILE YOUR LOGIC

A. Multiple Choice Questions:

1. An array is similar to
   - a. Conditions
   - b. Loops
   - c. Variable
   - d. None of the above

2. Which of the following brackets is used to make an array?
   - a. Square
   - b. Angle
   - c. Round
   - d. Curly

3. Which of the following modifications can be applied to a tuple?
   - a. Remove
   - b. Access
   - c. Change
   - d. Add

4. Which of the following cannot store the values with different data types?
   - a. Tuple
   - b. List
   - c. Array
   - d. All of the above

B. Tell whether the following statements are True/False:

1. A list can store values with different data types.

2. A tuple can be changed later in the program.

3. remove () is used to delete an item from a list.

4. append () changes the list item.

C. Fill in the blanks:

1. ______________ function removes an item using index value.

2. An array can store values with______________ data types.

3. The first item of a list has an index value as ______________ .

4. insert () is a ______________ function in python.

D. Short Answer type Questions:

1. What is an array?

2. How to make a list in python?

3. How to make a tuple in python?

4. How to sort an array?

E. Long Answer type Questions:

1. Explain data modification.
2. What is the advantage of using an array?
3. Briefly explain sorting of an array. How to sort in ascending and descending order?
4. Explain the differences between a list and a tuple.

Solve the code together

Complete the following blank commands in the program to add the names and marks obtained by the students. Both values should not be possible to be later changed in the program.

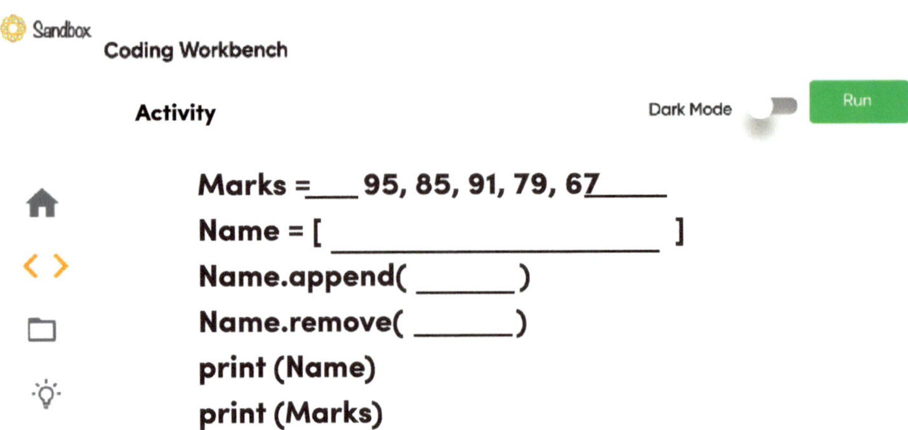

Hint: Make a tuple for unchangeable entries and use built-in functions.

Sam is creating a list of participants performing at the Children's Day celebration at his school. He needs the flexibility to add, remove and change the entries in the list. Help Sam create a list with the required functionality.

Create a list in the Scratch editor, where you have to take the age of 5 people and calculate the average of all the five ages. Write the algorithm of the program below.

Hint: Sum up all the list items and divide them by 5 to calculate the average.

Understand the code better

Jack is creating a 'Random Number game' in python where he wants to create a list of random numbers and print all of them in ascending order. He also wants to print the highest number among all of them.

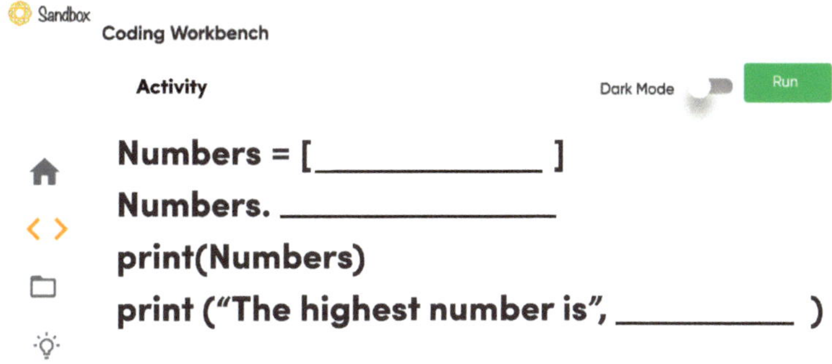

Hint: Use sorting of an array and the last index value to print the highest number.

DECODE THE CODE

SANDBOX CORNER

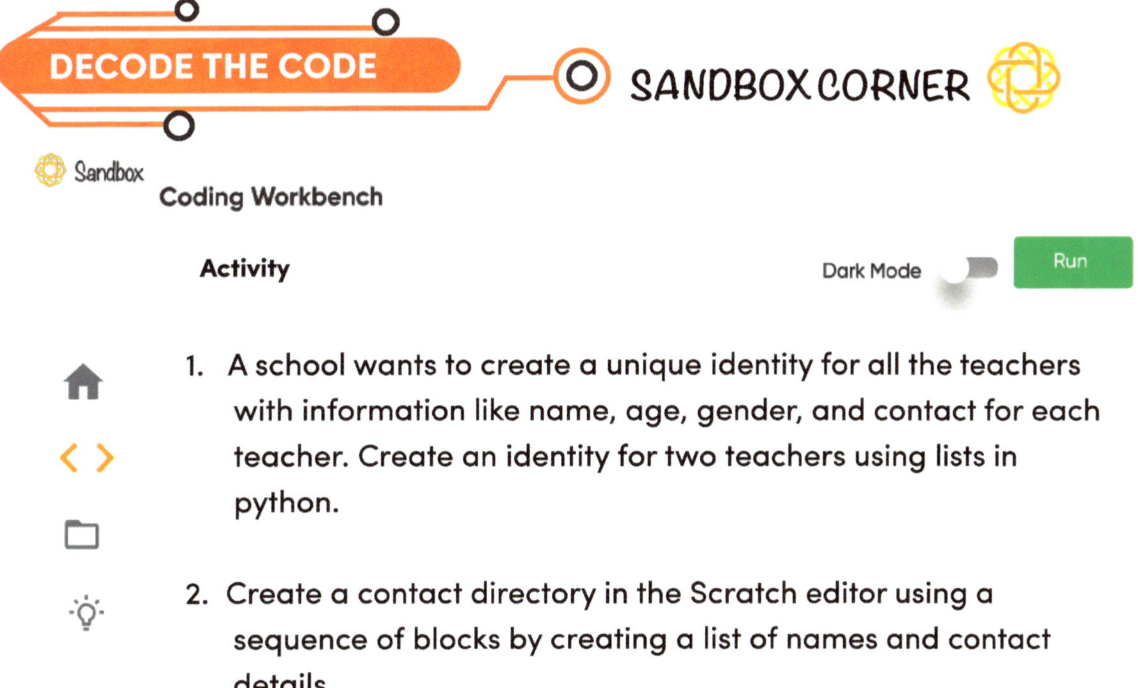

1. A school wants to create a unique identity for all the teachers with information like name, age, gender, and contact for each teacher. Create an identity for two teachers using lists in python.

2. Create a contact directory in the Scratch editor using a sequence of blocks by creating a list of names and contact details.

Master Worksheet – Section 3

Master Your Logic

A. Fill in the blanks

1. AND, OR & NOT are _______________ operators.

2. A ____________ loop repeats until the condition becomes TRUE.

3. A set of instructions that performs a specific task is known as____________.

4. An array can store values with _______________ data types.

5. _______________ brackets are used to create a tuple.

B. Match the columns

Column A	Column B
1. Tuples	A. It helps the program to take decisions.
2. Lists	B. A set of instructions reduces redundancy.
3. Functions	C. It cannot be modified once created.
4. Conditionals	D. It is a loop inside another loop.
5. Nested Loop	E. It can store multiple values with different data types.

Activity:

The algorithm given below is to check the greatest number among three numbers. Arrange the order of the algorithm and write it in the box to get the desired output.

a. Take inputs as A, B, C
b. If (A>C) print A else print C
c. Start
d. If (B>C) print B else print C
e. if (A>B) goto Step4 else goto step5
f. Stop

The correct sequence of algorithm

Activity:

Create a flowchart to print the square of a number "n" given by the user. The flowchart elements are given below, arrange all the elements using arrows to get the desired output.

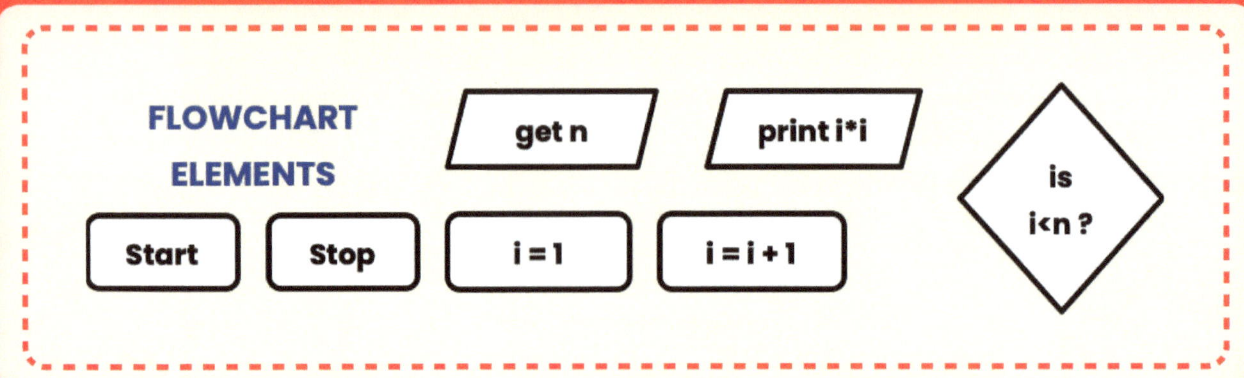

Make flowchart

Activity:

Write a python program that can reverse a list. The list of planet names is given and another list represents the desired output of the program.

GIVEN LIST:-　　　　　　　　　　Planets = ["Mercury", Venus, "Earth"]

DESIRED OUTPUT:-　　　　　　　　["Earth", Venus, "Mercury"]

Python program

Activity:
Create a flowchart to find the factorial of a number given by the user. Complete the
flowchart by adding the required statements like conditionals, print statements, etc.

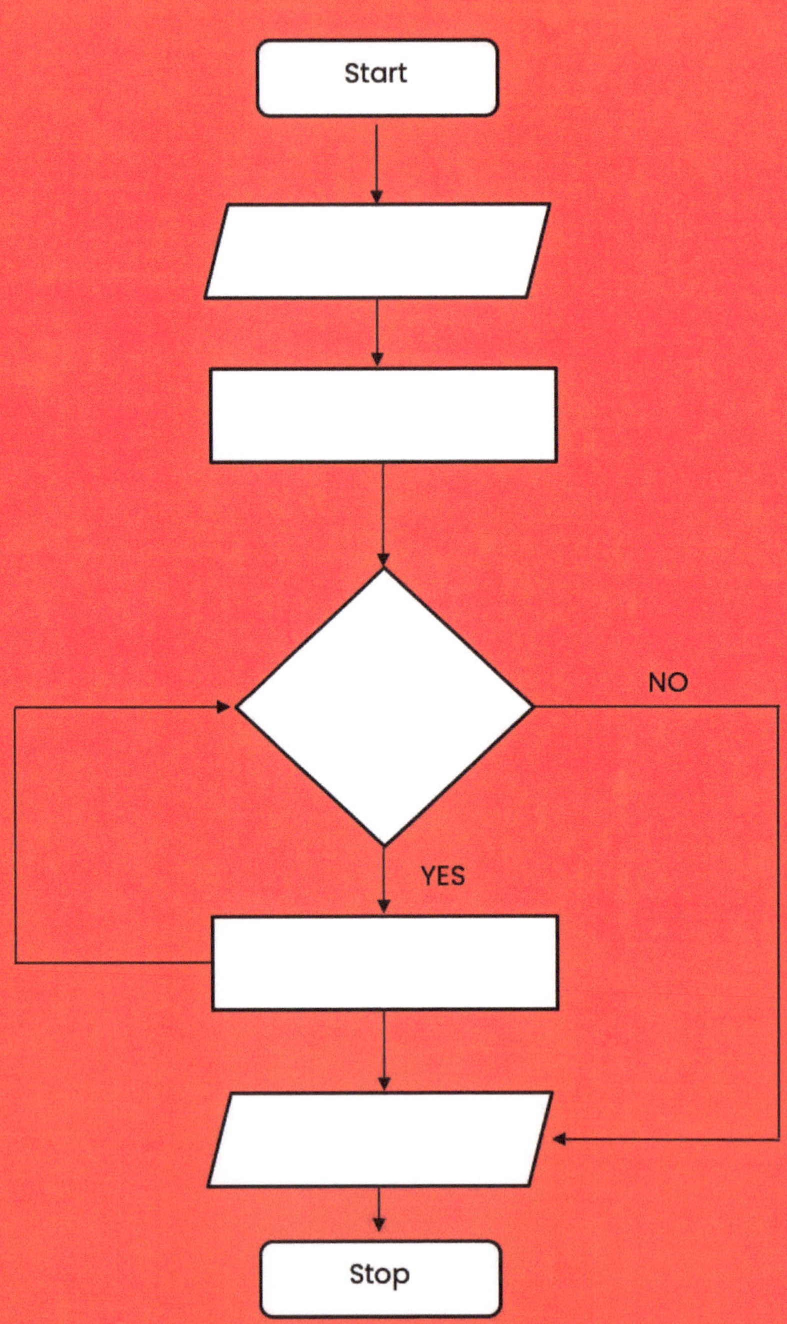
Start
NO
YES
Stop

ARTIFICIAL INTELLIGENCE & MACHINE LEARNING

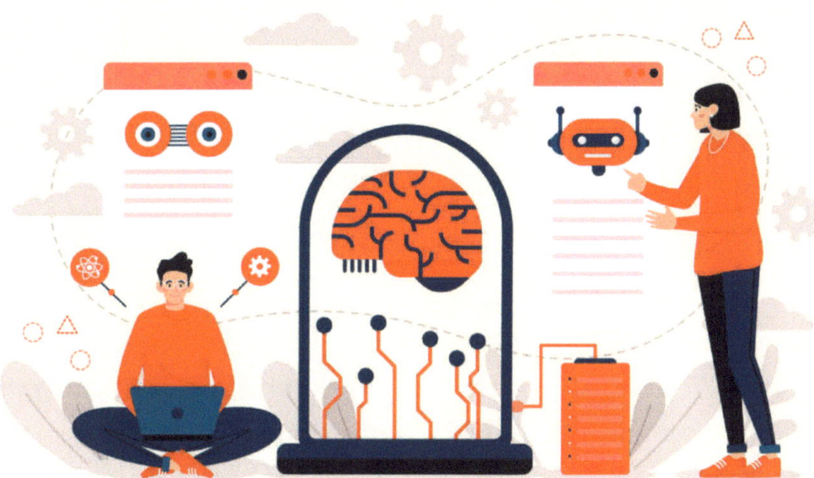

This section is a basic introduction for the kids to the world of artificial intelligence and machine learning

OVERVIEW

- Introduction to Artificial Intelligence
- History of Artificial Intelligence
- Difference between AI and ML
- Types of Artificial Intelligence
- Applications of Artificial Intelligence

REFRESH YOUR LOGIC!

- Machine learning is based on data.
- Machine learning finds patterns or connections in data.
- The accuracy of machine learning is dependent on the amount of data.

1. Introduction to Artificial Intelligence

Artificial Intelligence (AI) is the branch of computer science that makes or strives to make computers or machines do tasks which require similar level of intelligence as shown by human beings. This includes but is not limited to visual perception, speech recognition, language processing and decision making. With increasing capability and performance of machines, the field of artificial intelligence has been able to generate significant impetus.

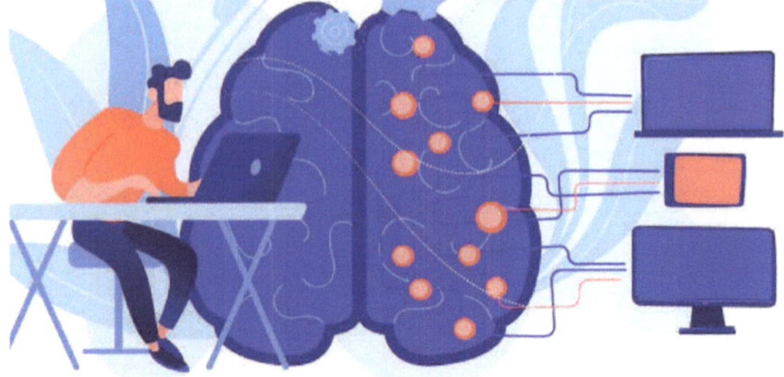

Fig 8.1

2. What is Artificial Intelligence?

John McCarthy, an American scientist and the father of AI, states artificial intelligence as the science and engineering of making intelligent machines, especially intelligent computer programs. It is a way of making computer-controlled machines like robots or software with intelligence similar to humans.

The system of AI is developed after studying how the human brain thinks, learns, decides, and works to solve a problem.

3. History of AI

The development of AI started with the intention of creating computers and machines which can behave and work as intelligently as a human does.

By the 1950s, Alan Turing, known as the father of computer science, raised a question among scientists - "Can computers think?". Post which, he developed a technique called the "Turing test". In this test, humans try to distinguish text responses generated by humans and computers. As per this test, if the computer is able to have a conversation that is indistinguishable from a human conversation, it will be called intelligent.

In the 1980s, AI was able to provide intelligence to computer systems. These computer systems which could simulate human intelligence were called **Expert Systems**. There has been continuous growth in the development of AI after this.

4. Difference between AI and ML

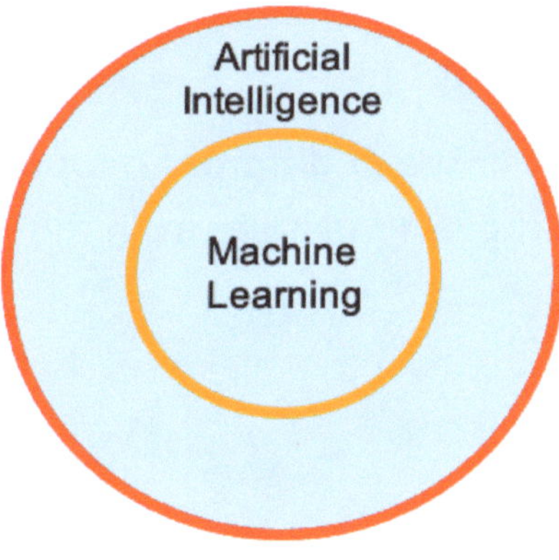

Fig 8.2

Machine learning trains computers to make better decisions creating an artificially intelligent system. An artificially intelligent system uses machine learning tools to develop its intelligence. All machine learning system counts as AI but not all AI counts as machine learning. So machine learning is a subset of artificial intelligence.

Artificial intelligence(AI)	Machine learning(ML)
• AI is the ability of computers to show intelligence. • AI is the decision-making power of computers. • It is the way to solve complex problems. • AI uses ML to gain intelligence. • AI is used to find optimal solutions. • The objective is to increase the chance of success and not accuracy.	• ML is the way to make computers capable of thinking. • ML helps computers to learn from the data provided. • It is the way to gather knowledge from data. • ML is a subset of AI. • ML gives results based on data (might not be an optimal solution). • The objective is to increase accuracy, but it does not care about success.

Let's train a robot to identify the nose of the human body using artificial intelligence by providing images to learn.

Step 1. Take some pictures of the noses of different people. Mark each nose with a red square, as shown below. This is the data used to train the computer.

Step 2. Using a red rectangle, we have specified that the area under the red rectangle indicates the nose.

Step 3. Now, verify whether the AI-powered robot has detected the correct position of the nose in the following picture or not.

Image 1 ____

Image 2 ____

Image 3 ____

5. Types of Artificial Intelligence

On the basis of capabilities, AI can be divided into the following three types:

- **Weak AI**
- **General AI**
- **Super AI**

5.1 Weak Artificial Intelligence

Weak AI helps turn large amounts of data into usable information by detecting patterns and making predictions. Weak AI, otherwise referred to as Artificial Narrow Intelligence (ANI), describes the algorithms that can complete some predefined function. This is the only type of AI that exists at present. The algorithms divide data and then make decisions based on the patterns in data.

It's called weak because it has limited functionality. Weak AI accomplishes specific tasks that require human intelligence and decision-making.
Some practical examples of weak AI are given below.

- **Digital voice assistants (Siri, Alexa)**

Digital voice assistants such as Siri and Alexa are some common examples of weak AI that are widely used. They recognize words in the speech and respond to queries instantly.

- **Recommendation engines**

Online video platforms (like Youtube) suggesting what video you should watch next or retail websites offering you helpful advice about what else you might be interested in purchasing are all recommendation engines and are real life examples of narrow or weak AI.

- **Search engines**

Google and other search engines are also examples of weak AI. When you type something to search, the algorithm classifies it into different words and shows the matching results.

- **Chatbots**

Most organizations use automated texting software that replies to general queries (like a human can do) and is called a chatbot. Chatbot uses AI to find the best possible answer using predefined answers in its system.

- **Semi-Autonomous vehicles**

Semi-autonomous vehicles are also examples of weak AI. The AI uses an algorithm with predefined functions to perform a specific task. Weak AI doesn't have full cognitive abilities like a human brain, so it is trained to avoid road hazards.

5.2 Artificial General Intelligence

Artificial General Intelligence (AGI) also referred to as strong AI or deep AI, is the ability of machines to think, learn, and apply intelligence to solve complex problems. Strong AI uses a theory of mind AI framework to recognize other intelligent systems' emotions, beliefs, and thought processes. The next-generation AGI is a machine with general intelligence that can solve problems like a human being.

Some examples of AGI are given below.

- **Alter and adapt to changing circumstances**

General AI machines will be able to adapt themselves as they encounter changing or new circumstances. Narrow AI is only able to respond to variables/circumstances that were programmed into algorithms.

- **Solve a puzzle**

AI algorithms have been created which have competed and won video games and chess matches. Those successes are examples of AI following patterns and programs. When machines can solve a puzzle on its own, general AI will be achieved.

- **Beyond mathematical equations**

Narrow AI proved in many ways that many of the problems we solve as humans are just mathematical equations. When a machine can go beyond mathematical equations to general problem solving, machines will have human intelligence.

5.3 Artificial Super Intelligence

Artificial Super Intelligence (ASI) is a type of AI that surpasses human intelligence and can perform any task better than a human. Although the existence of ASI is still hypothetical, the decision-making and problem-solving capabilities of such systems are expected to be far superior to those of human beings. Typically, an ASI system can think, solve puzzles, make judgments, and take decisions independently.

Tech Fact

OpenAI is used to make the system highly autonomous which writes the AI algorithms in python programming language.

Machines with super-intelligence are self-aware and can think of ways that humans cannot. ASI finds application in all domains of human interests like maths, science, arts, sports, medicine, marketing, or even emotional relations. An ASI system can perform all tasks that a human can perform – from defining a new mathematical theorem for a problem to exploring physics law while venturing into outer space.

ASI systems can quickly understand, analyze, and process circumstances to take actions. As a result, the decision-making and problem-solving capabilities of super-intelligent machines are expected to be more precise than humans.

6. Limitations of Artificial Intelligence

While the field of AI can be revolutionary in terms of what it can enable, it also comes with its own limitations and challenges:

- **High cost**

Developing a machine that can reflect human intelligence requires plenty of resources and time and hence is highly costly.

- **Unemployment**

AI-powered robots are utilized in manufacturing to increase work efficiency. As a result, human employment is decreasing.

- **No ethics**

Integrating AI with ethics and moral logic is difficult. As AI lacks moral values, concerns around unethical usage of AI systems are increasing rapidly.

- **Emotionless**

AI does not have any emotions like humans. Its work is only based on logic. So it can't be fully trusted like humans.

7. Real–life Applications of Artificial Intelligence

Sophia

Sophia is the first **humanoid robot** developed by **Hanson Robotics** company. It was completed on February 14, 2016. After one month, it made its first appearance in public in Texas, US. It gave many high-profile interviews. It was given the citizenship of Saudi Arabia and was also the first robot to get citizenship of any country. It is able to imitate human gestures and facial expressions like humans and can learn on its own. However, it can only discuss some predefined topics.

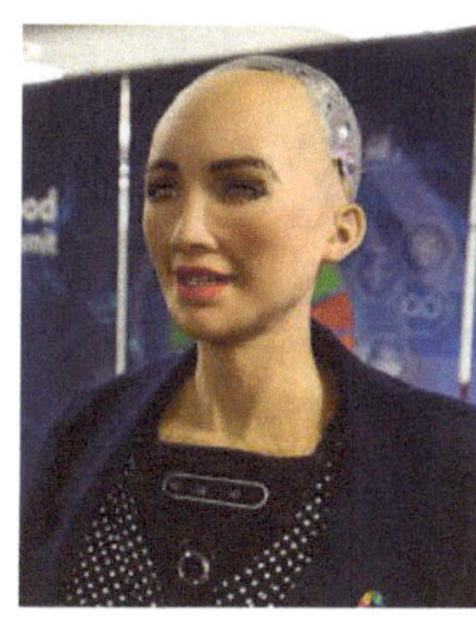

Fig 8.2

Spot

Spot is a four-legged and dog-like robot made for commercial purposes by Boston Dynamics, a robotics company.
It was revealed on June 16, 2016, and made available to the public in 2019. Its actions can be programmed using an application. It was used by SpaceX to inspect the area around the launchpad of the spaceship.
Boston Dynamics is also working on many commercial robots and humanoid robots.

Fig 8.3

Waymo

Waymo is an American self-driving car company operating in Arizona. This company was one of the google AI projects. This company introduced its self-driving cars to the public in October 2020. At that time, it was the only company that operated self-driving cars without backup drivers. This company later developed autonomous delivery vans and an autonomous tractor-trailer system for long-distance delivery and logistics. Later on, many other companies started developing hybrid and fully autonomous cars.

Fig 8.4

Smart Home assistants

Smart home assistants are devices that can assist you like humans, using AI. You may have used a virtual assistant on your phone to call someone or open an app. These assistants are interfaced directly with a device, capable of voice detection and reply in the human voice, and also can control smart devices at home.

Amazon has built a virtual assistant, "Alexa" and interfaced it with a device named "Amazon Echo". It can interact like humans and can help with many tasks.

Fig 8.5

These are many other examples of AI-powered devices. The efficiency and accuracy of AI devices are increasing day by day.

REFRESH YOUR LOGIC!

- AI is the ability of computer systems to show intelligence like humans.
- AI was introduced in 1956.
- AI can be used in many robots and many other fields.
- Many companies are building AI robots and devices.

Summary: LET'S PACK OUR STUFF!

- Artificial intelligence gives power to computers to show intelligence like humans.
- Computer systems that can show intelligence are called expert systems.
- Machine learning is a part of artificial intelligence.
- Artificial Intelligence is of three types – weak, general and super artificial intelligence.
- Using machine learning, AI is able to predict better results.

DID YOU KNOW

In AI, we create artificial neural networks which create interconnections between data groups. These networks work like neurons in the human brain.

- Sophia is the first AI humanoid robot.
- Spot is a four-legged AI robot based on canines.
- Waymo built the first autonomous car which could operate without a backup driver.
- Smart home assistants are devices that interact like humans.

COMPILE YOUR LOGIC

A. Multiple Choice Questions:

1. AI is the ability of computers to
   - a. think
   - b. talk
   - c. walk
   - d. none of the above

2. ML in AI helps to predict better
   - a. results.
   - b. problem.
   - c. faces.
   - d. none of the above.

3. The first humanoid AI robot was
   - a. Spot
   - b. Sputnik
   - c. Aryabhatta
   - d. Sophia

4. Spot design is based on
   - a. fish
   - b. birds
   - c. canines
   - d. snakes

B. Tell whether the following statements are True/False:

1. AI cannot identify faces.

2. ML and AI have zero connection.

3. Sophia has citizenship in Saudi Arabia.

4. Waymo is a four-legged robot.

C. Fill in the blanks: 

1. Spot has ______________ legs.

2. ML is a ______________ of AI.

3. AI helps machines to show intelligence like ______________ .

4. ______________ is the virtual assistant of Amazon company.

D. Short Answer type Questions: 

1. What is Artificial Intelligence?

2. Name three types of AI.

3. What is the use of ML in AI?

4. What are the applications of AI?

E. Long Answer type Questions:

1. List the differences between AI and ML.

2. Explain Weak Artificial Intelligence with examples.

3. Explain Artificial General Intelligence with examples.

4. Explain Artificial Super Intelligence with examples.

STEP UP YOUR CODE GAME

Solve the code together

Your friend is making an AI robot. He wants to train the robot to recognize an apple in the fruit basket.

Step 1. Mark the circle on the apples in the fruit bucket to train.

Step 2: ____

Step 3: ____

Step 4: ____

Sam wants to train an AI-powered camera to identify the letter "K" written in different handwritings, but he doesn't know how AI is trained to perform tasks. Help him by showing the steps on how he can train an AI camera.

You receive many spam emails that contain unsecured links. Write some spam links to train AI to detect spam emails.

Step 1. If an email contains insecure links.

Link 1. _______________________________

Link 2. _______________________________

Link 3. _______________________________

Step 2. _______________________________________

Step 3. Verify the working of AI software.

Master Worksheet – Section 4

Master Your Logic

A. Fill in the blanks

1. Chatbots use _________________ AI.

2. Super AI can surpass _______________ intelligence.

3. AI uses ______________ to develop intelligence in a computer system.

4. High cost is ______________ of AI.

5. _______________ can simulate human intelligence.

B. Match the columns

Column A	Column B
1. Sophia	A. Voice assistant
2. Spot	B. Autonomous Car
3. Waymo	C. Created Sophia
4. Siri	D. Humanoid robot
5. Hanson Robotics	E. Four-legged robot

Activity:

Peter wants to train AI to arrange these images in the correct order. Help Peter arrange these images in the correct order for making a burger in the given box below:

Items- Milk bottle, Chips, Sprite, Chocolate, Candy, Coke, Pepsi, Amul milk, Oats, Maggi, Corn flakes,

	1.	2.	3.
1.			
2.			
3.			
4.			

Rules- You have to arrange similar items in the same row.

Activity:
AI can be used to find the differences between the given two images. Can you also find the differences?

Difference:
1.
2.
3.
4.
5.

I. Sam – "Hi"
  Voice assistant reply – "__________________"
II. Sam – "How are you?"
  Voice assistant reply – "________________"
III. Sam –
Voice assistant reply – " ________________"

Chapter 1

MCQ:

1(c), 2(c), 3(b), 4(d)

True or False

1(a), 2(a), 3(b), 4(a)

Fill in the blanks

1:Hacking, 2: Virus, 3: Phishing , 4: HyperText Transfer, 5: Protocol

Chapter 2

MCQ:

1(c), 2(c), 3(a), 4(b)

True or False

1(b), 2(b),3(b), 4(a)

Fill in the blanks

1: sorting, 2: noise, 3: discretization , 4: analysis

Chapter 3

MCQ:

1(c), 2(b), 3(d), 4(a)

True or False

1(a), 2(a), 3(b), 4(a)

Fill in the blanks

1: Form, 2: left to right, 3: border-style, 4: div

Chapter 4

MCQ

1(b), 2(c), 3(a), 4(d)

True or False

1(b), 2(b), 3(a), 4(b)

Fill in the blanks

1: padding, 2: Nav Bar , 3: *, 4: background-size

Chapter 5

MCQ

1(a), 2(c), 3(d), 4(b)

True or False

1(b), 2(a), 3(b), 4(a)

Fill in the blanks

1: nested , 2: true, 3: for, 4: Pass

Chapter 6

MCQ

1(c), 2(d), 3(c), 4(a)

True or False

1(b), 2(b), 3(a), 4(a)

Fill in the blanks

1: output , 2: Functions, 3: Parameter, 4: set

Chapter 7

MCQ

1(c), 2(a), 3(b), 4(c)

True or False

1(a), 2(b), 3(a), 4(b)

Fill in the blanks

1: pop , 2: similar , 3: zero, 4: built-in

Chapter 8

MCQ

1(a), 2(a), 3(d), 4(c)

True or False

1(b), 2(b), 3(a), 4(b)

Fill in the blanks

1: four , 2: sub-part , 3: human , 4: Alexa

Answer key for Master Worksheet 1

Fill in the blanks

1: Computer Virus, 2: Ethical, 3: Https, 4: Host, 5: Data transformation.

Match the columns

1-E, 2-A, 3-D, 4-B, 5-C

Answer key for Master Worksheet 2

Fill in the blanks

1: Asterisk (*), 2: background-image , 3: anchor , 4: four, 5: Submit

Match the columns

1-D, 2-E, 3-A, 4-B, 5-C

Answer key for Master Worksheet 3

Fill in the blanks

1: Logical , 2: While, 3: Function, 4: similar , 5: Round

Match the columns

1-C, 2-E, 3-B, 4-A, 5-D

Answer key for Master Worksheet 4

Fill in the blanks

1: Weak, 2: Human, 3: Machine learning, 4: Limitations, 5: Expert system

Match the columns

1-D, 2-E, 3-B, 4-A, 5-C

Internet Safety

 **Never click on pop-up ads and if you end up clicking, close the browser immediately**

 **Do not click on any link or fill in any personal information on links sent by an unknown number**

 **Make strong passwords using mix of uppercase, lowercase, numerics and characters**

 **Do not open spammy links or download any software or files sent by an unknown email**

 **Do not click or sign up on unsecured website links as your details could be hacked**

 **If you receive any spam calls, do not provide any personal information. Also, report that number and block it.**

 **Spammers use look-like official email addresses, verify the email address before proceeding further**

 **Don't download software from an unauthorised website as they could install malware onto your device**

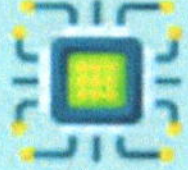 **Keep your anti-virus software up to date and always ON.**

Why should kids learn to code?

⭐ Coding helps kids develop problem solving and critical thinking skills

⭐ Coding increases resilience and the ability to keep trying till one succeeds

⭐ Coding enhances mathematical and logical skills

⭐ Kids learn to face and solve difficult problems, leading to enhancement in self confidence

⭐ Learning to code is like learning a new language - you get better with time - hence starting at an early age helps

⭐ Coding encourages hands-on learning, do-it-yourself attitude and creative thinking capability

⭐ Coding requires kids to be resourceful and work with other students to solve problems for better output

⭐ Knowing how to code helps prepare kids for majority of the jobs of the future

Ethics in Computer Science

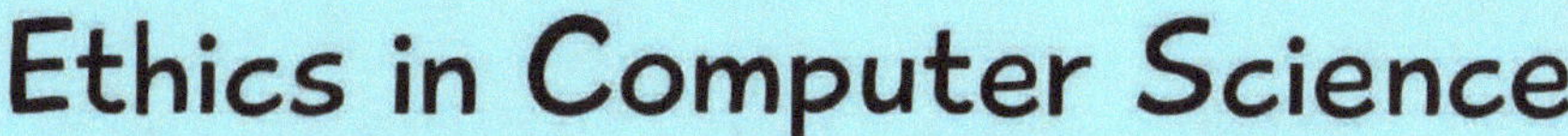

- Use creative commons or publicly available media only, and refrain from using material which was created by others (without mentioning)

- Always consider the licences on computational artifacts that you wish to use.

- Protect the interests of innovators and do not engage in patent trolls or abuse patent laws for financial gain, as it is someone else's intellectual property.

- Take permission from the user before collecting the data through automated processes that may not be evident to users.

- In a dilemma, always put an individual's right to privacy first as it is a fundamental right.

- Do not bypass a system's security, and do not try to install software without having to complete the registration and authentication requirements.

- Be open and honest with the stakeholders, fully disclosing all relevant system capabilities, restrictions, and potential issues.

- Make efforts to develop systems or technologies that are as inclusive and accessible as feasible.

Secure Your Privacy

Like it is critical to follow guidelines to ensure internet safety, it is also important to be cautious and follow sharing guidelines while using social networking sites (e.g. facebook, instagram, snapchat, etc.) and messaging apps (whatsapp, messenger, etc.) as well. Over-sharing of personal information or sharing sensitive information with unknown people can put you at high risk of cyber-attacks.

Use the below worksheet to test your level of awareness with respect to sharing information over social networks and messenger apps. For each question, select who all you would share the information with. Note that there can be multiple correct answers. You have to select from the following options - parents, friends, public and no one.

1. Your personal chats on a messaging app:

a. 

b. 

c. 

d. 

2. The PIN number of the debit card:

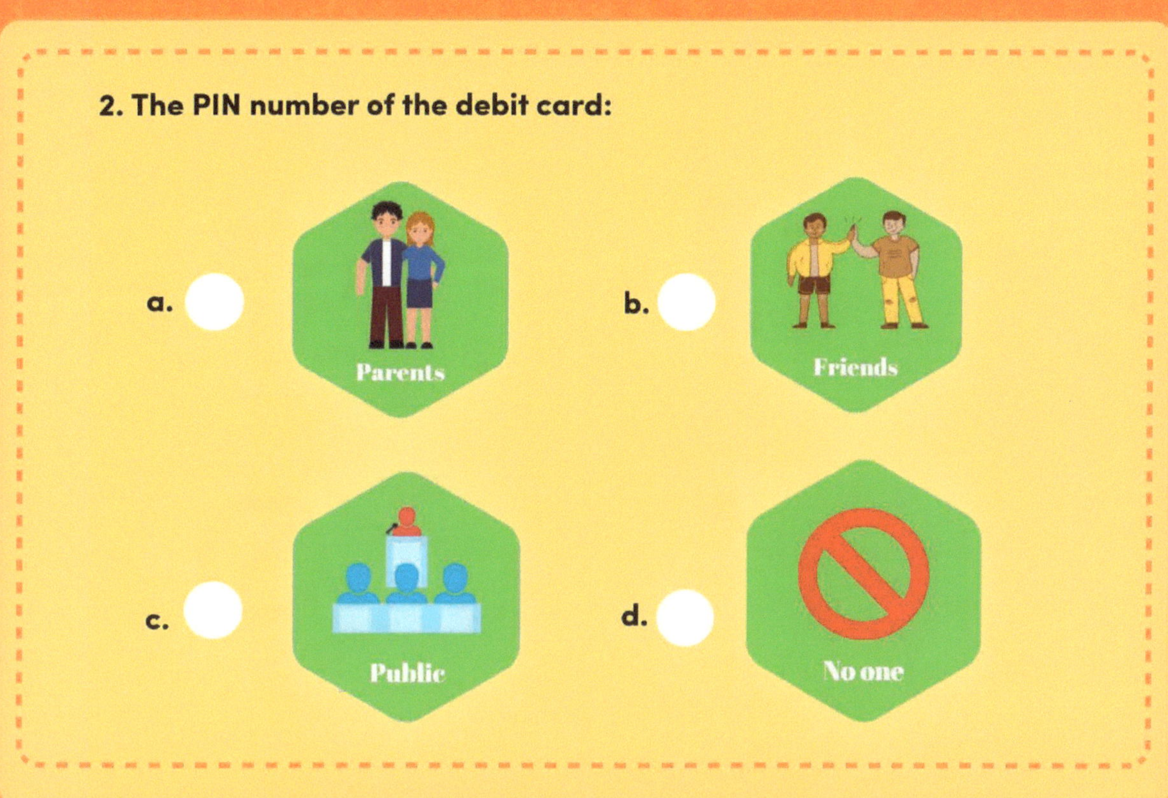

a. b. c. d.

3. Details of flight tickets:

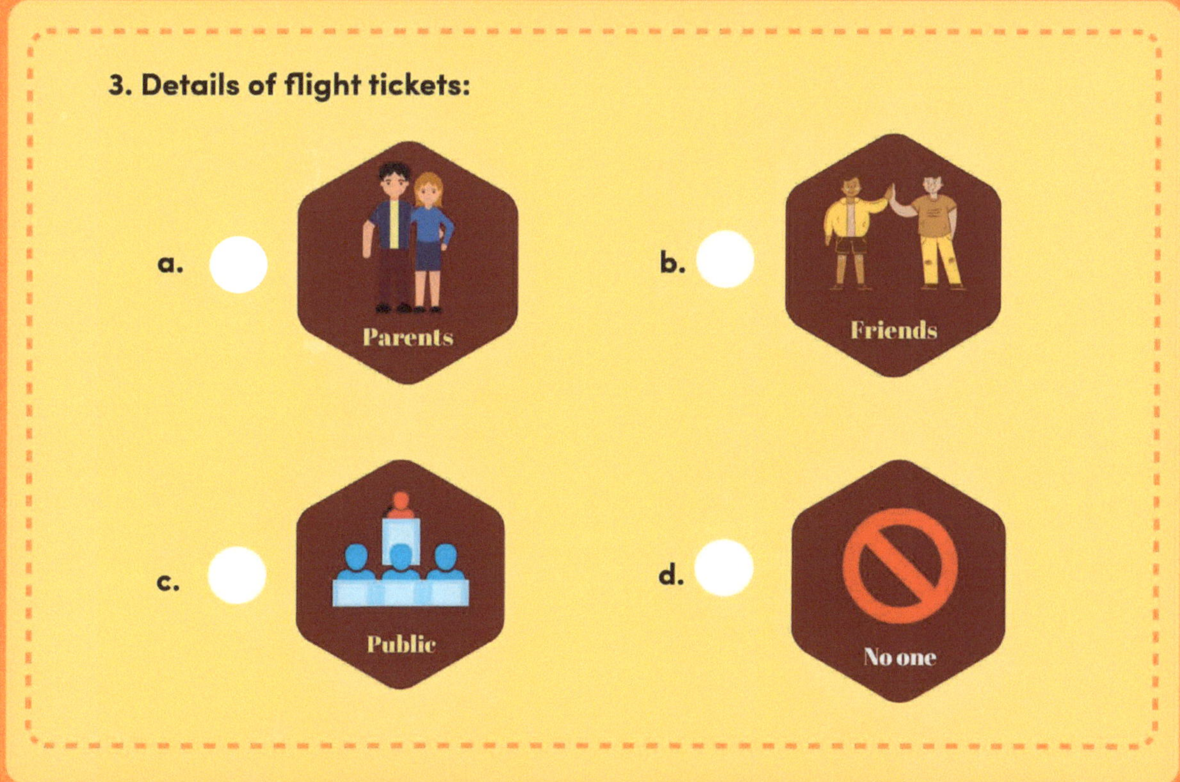

a. b. c. d.

4. An inspirational quote:

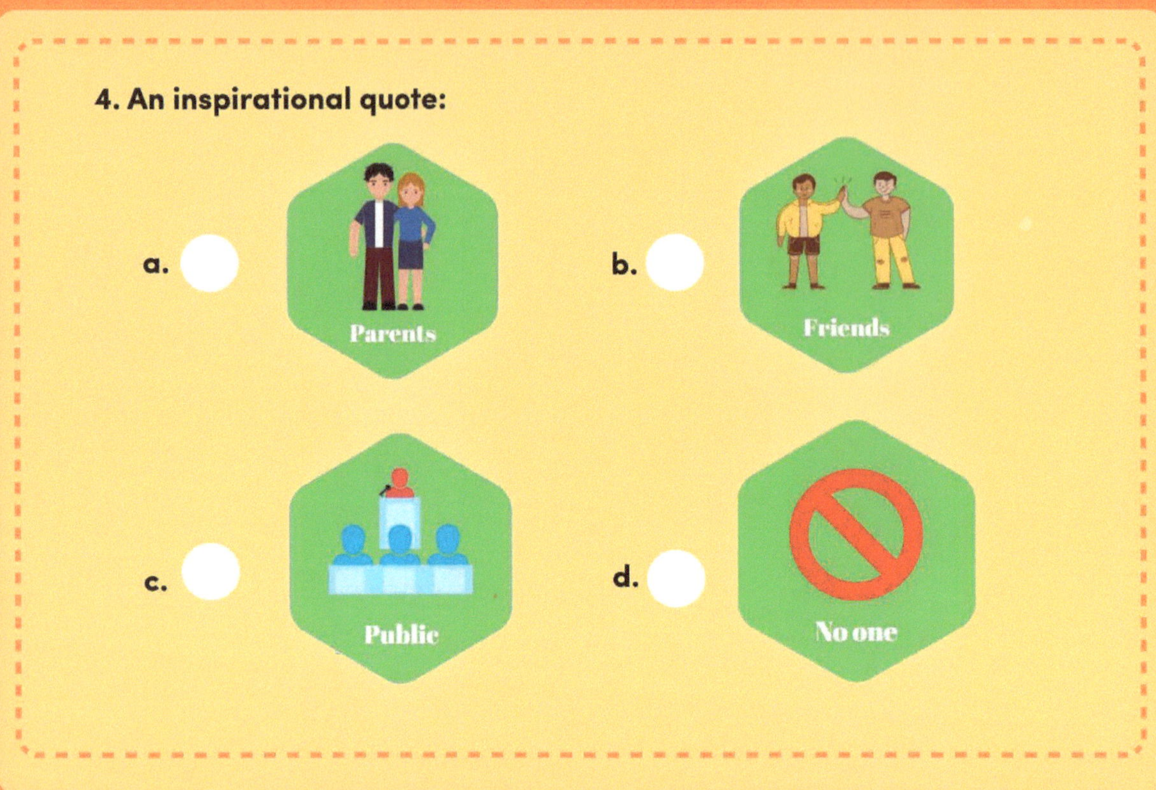

5. The screen lock pattern of your mobile:

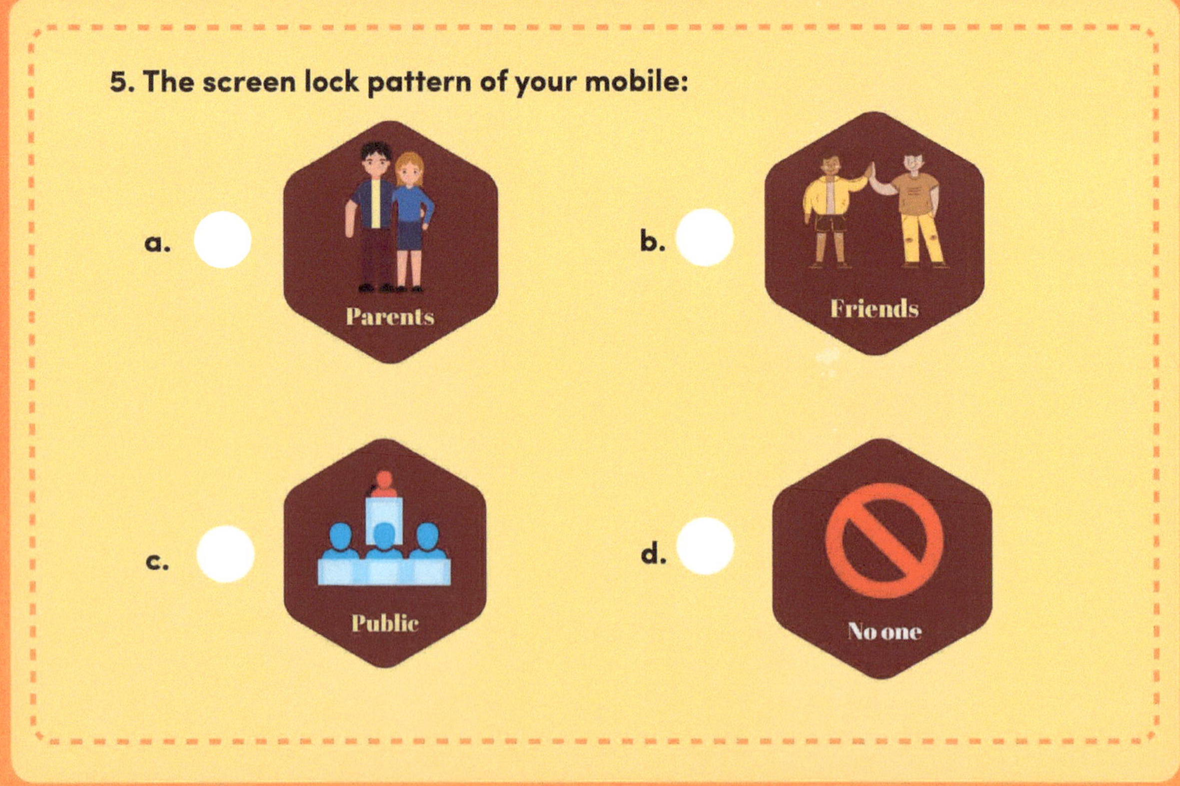

6. A review of a restaurant:

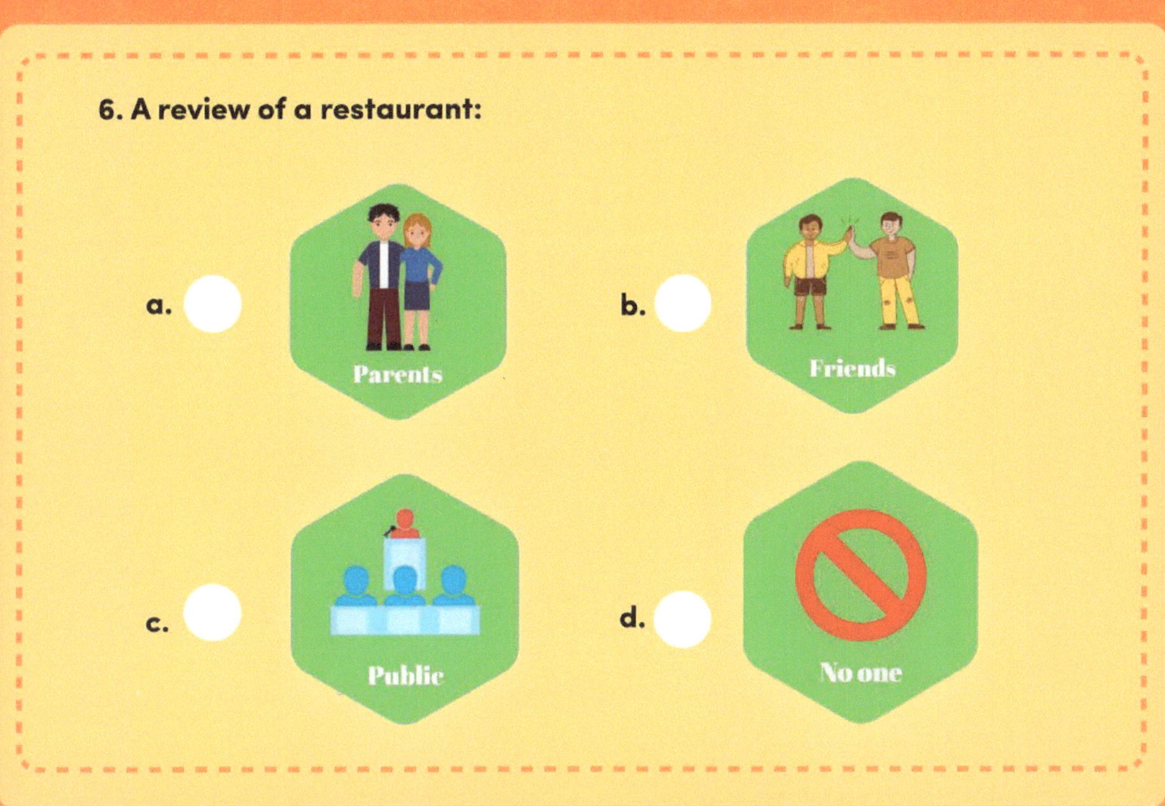

7. The password of your email/social media account:

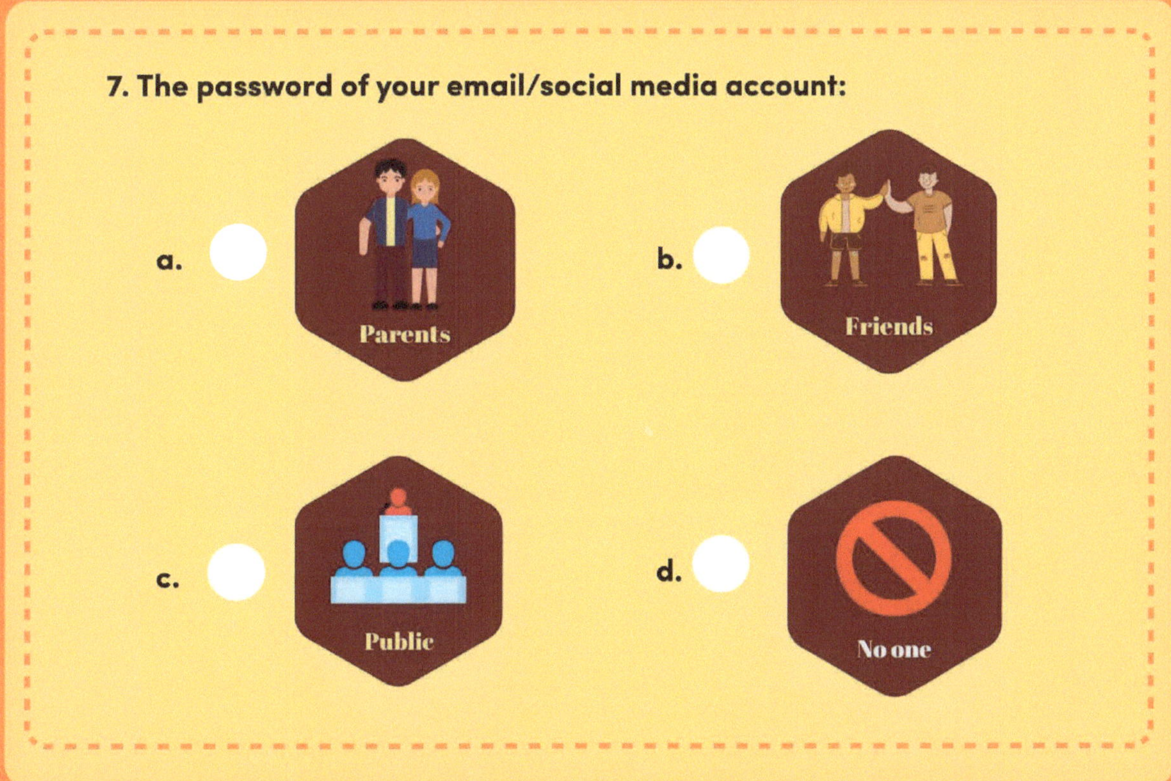

8. Your academic achievement certificate:

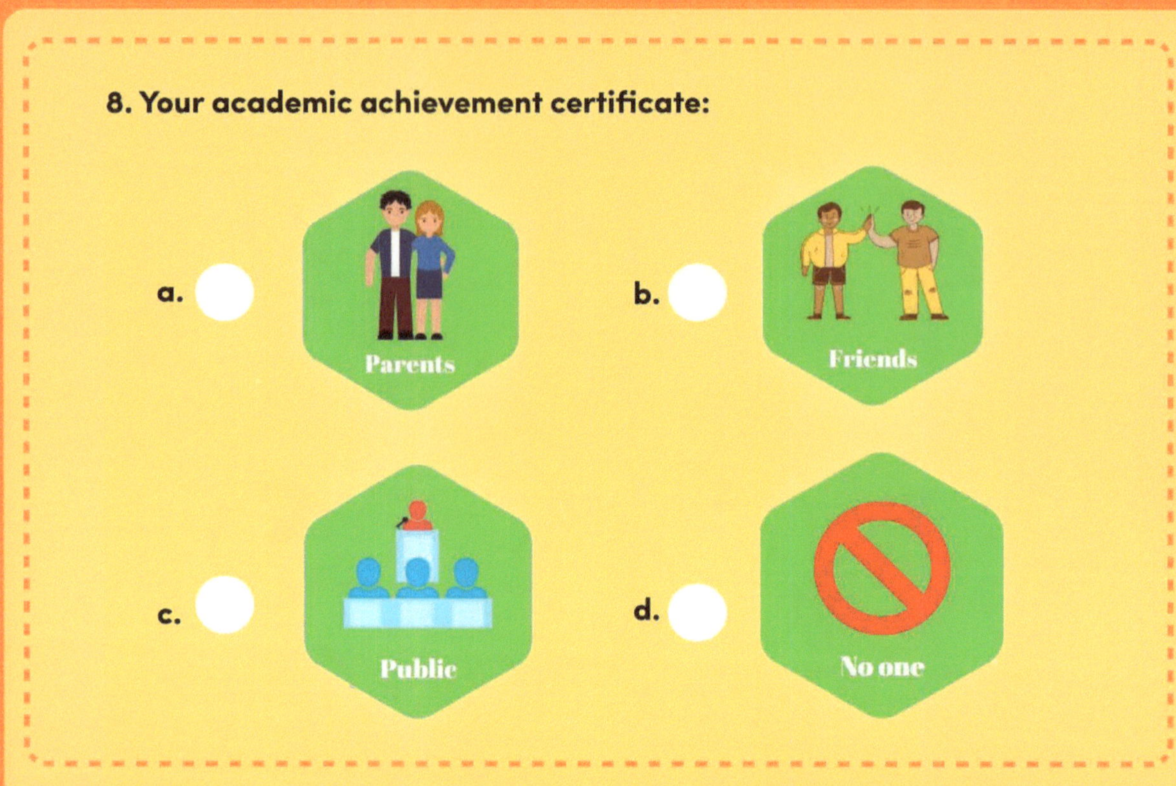

9. Parent's credit card details:

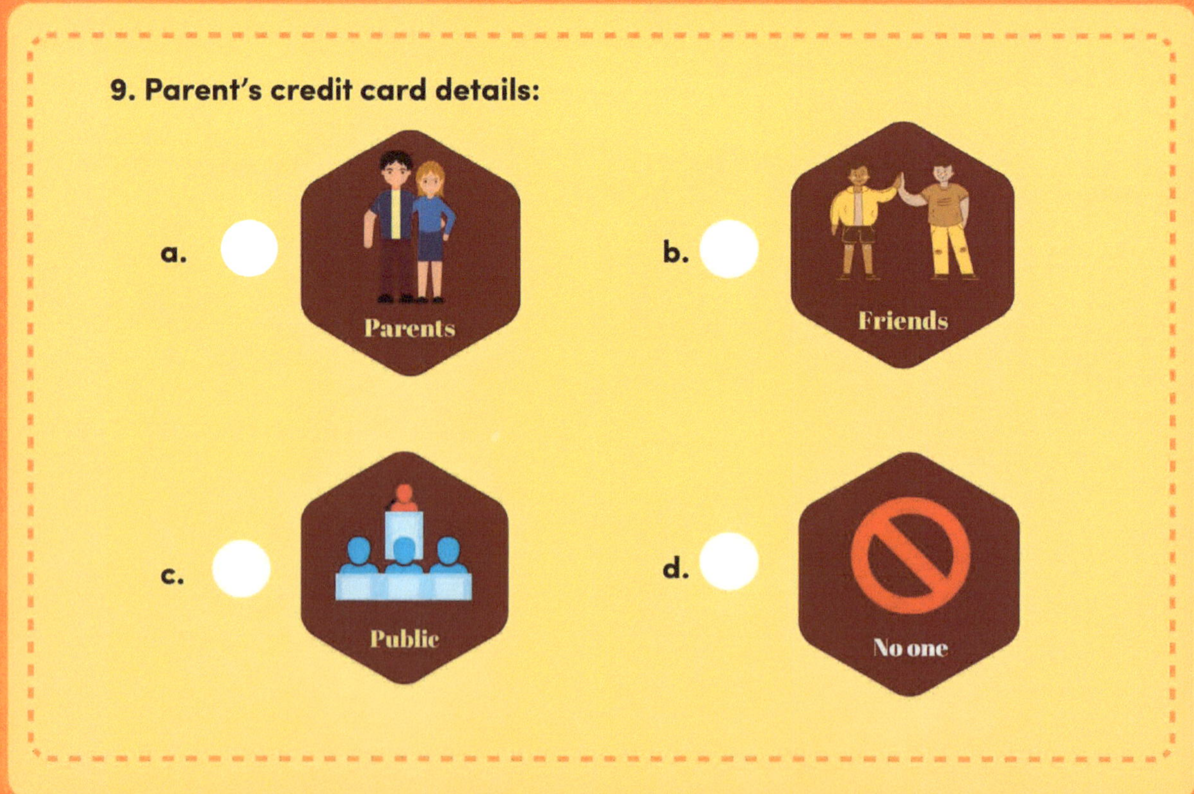

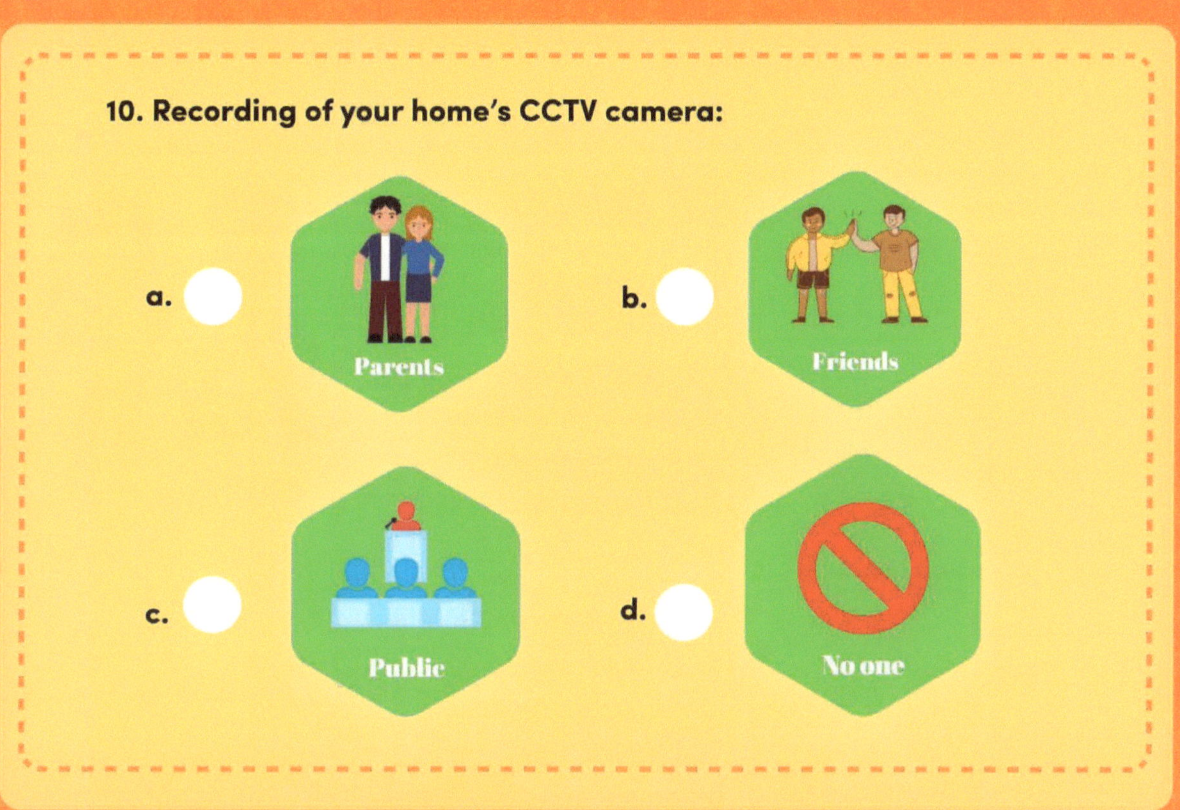

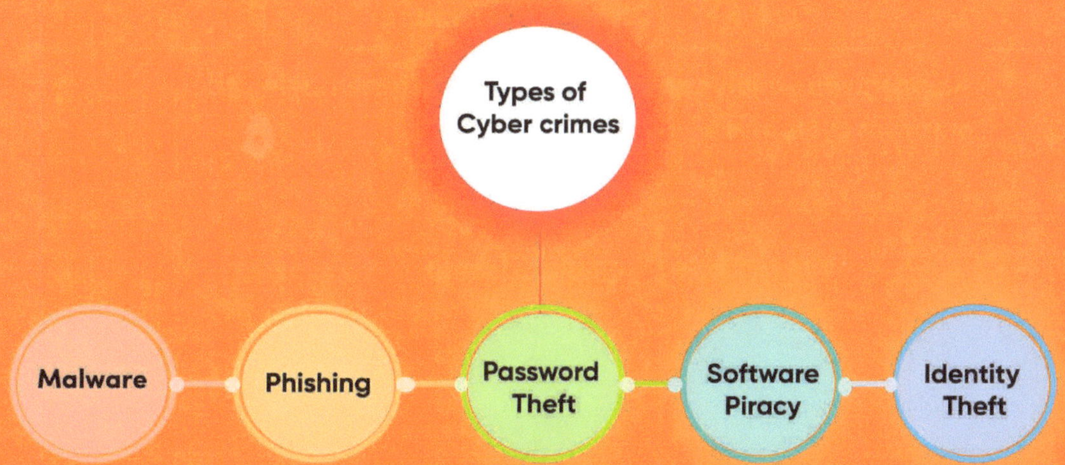

And many more...

Beware!

Test your skills

1. Which of the following is used to print the tuple "fruit"?

a. print("fruit")

b. print(tuple)

c. print(fruit)

d. tuple(fruit)

2. Function remove() is used to–

a. Change the list

b. print("fruit")

c. Delete the list item

d. Change the list item

3. The program which can replicate itself after entering the computer system is

a. Virus

b. Spreadsheet

c. Adware

d. malware

4. Which AI is used to make search engines?

a. Weak AI

b. Super AI

c. General AI

d. None of the above

5. Items in a list can be-

a. Change

b. Accessed

c. Deleted

d. All of the above

6. The person which accesses data without permission.

a. Hacker

b. Operator

c. Instructor

d. Helper

7. A function parameter works as a/an-

a. Array

b. Variable

c. Data type

d. Operator

8. =MATCH() function is used for

a. Indexing

b. Sorting

c. Formatting

d. Matching

9. Which of the following is used to add an item in a list?

a. append()

b. insert()

c. Both a and b

d. None of the above

10. Spot is the product of

a. Tesla

b. Boston Dynamics

c. Waymo

d. Hanson Robotics

11. Which of the following is an ID selector in CSS?

a. .class{}

b. @class{}

c. *{}

d. #class{}

12. Which of the following detail you should not share with anyone?

a. Name

b. Address

c. Password

d. None of the above

1. C, 2. C, 3. A, 4. A, 5. D, 6. A,
7. B, 8. D, 9. C, 10. B, 11. D, 12. C.

www.ingramcontent.com/pod-product-compliance
Lightning Source LLC
Chambersburg PA
CBHW042125150726
48005CB00029B/221